When you
are balanced
and when you
listen and attend
to the needs of
your body, mind,
and spirit, your
natural beauty comes out.
>> Christy Turlington

the
natural
issue

Editor & Publisher
Brigid Danziger

Editing & Proofreading
Michael Dober

Writers
Kelly Barendt
Brigid Danziger
Carmen Myer
Kate Wright

Sponsored and Produced by
Math Giraffe, LLC

Follow On Instagram
@snowdaymagazine

Contact Us
editor@snowdaymagazine.com

Advertising
media@snowdaymagazine.com

Website
SNOWDAYMAGAZINE.COM

Photography
Front cover and this page:
Lauren McGee @laurenandloft
Back cover: Liv @wild.and.play

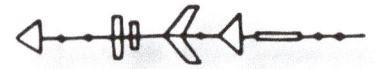

8

Natural Inspiration

Why humans need a daily dose of the outdoors, how to find your local trails, and tips for bringing nature's powerful effect into your classroom

60

Natural Homes

Get the beauty of the earth's most gorgeous materials in an affordable way through these small high-impact touches

30

Natural Learning

Adapting Reggio-Inspired Methods for your own students' needs

12

Natural Classrooms

Inspiration from teachers who are working to bring the joys, textures, and experiences of nature into their learning environments

bonus pages to copy & use 114

FEATURES

24

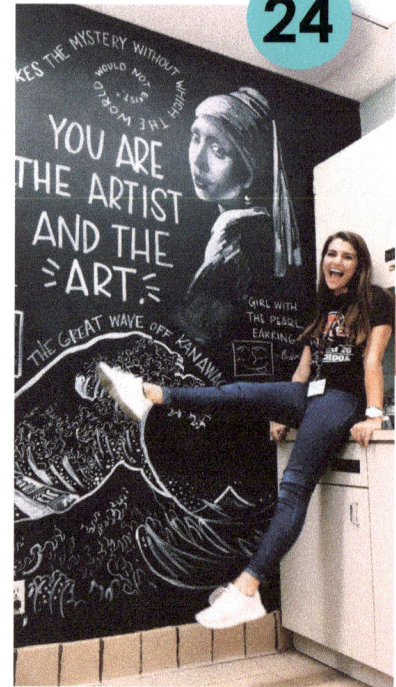

Teacher Feature:
Kristen Yann

Tell me, what is it you plan to do with your one wild and precious life?
>> Mary Oliver

98

Macrame Makes a Comeback

86

Building Habits

106

Mess Remedies for Teachers

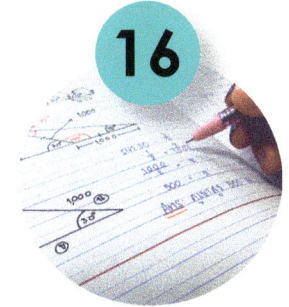

16

Note Taking: Digital vs. By Hand

108

5 Ways to Style It

112

Candles: You're Not Burning them Right

CONTENTS

50

Ingenuity, Invention, & Inspiration

80

Clipboards Tips & Tricks

74

Tackling Terra Cotta

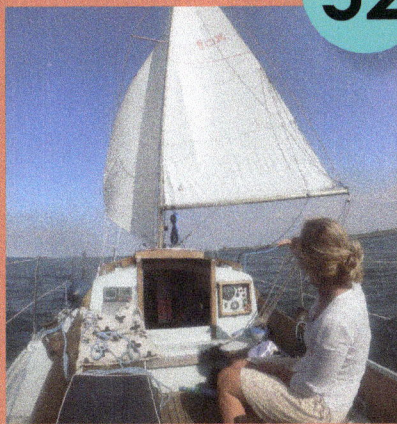

52

Sailing the World: A Teacher's Dream

34

Natural Lessons & Materials

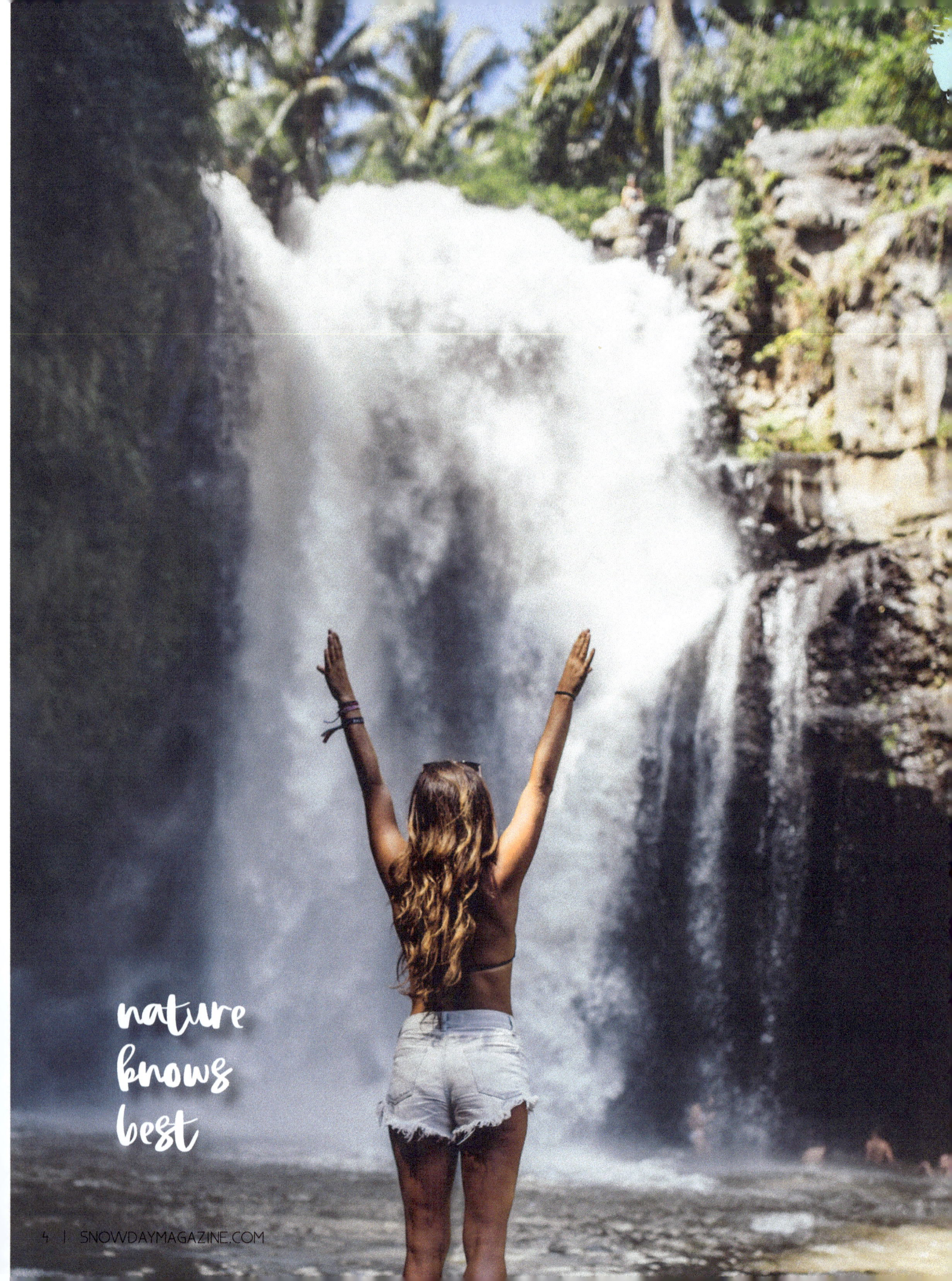

nature
knows
best

FROM THE EDITOR...

I've been captivated lately by the fact that **you just can't beat nature**. This idea has popped up when choosing materials for home projects, thinking about the textures of things we touch every day, and even navigating the process of trying to find a natural deodorant that won't have any potential to increase my chances of breast cancer. A few months ago, when my daughter complained that her face did not look like the flawless Disney princesses in her book, I was lucky enough to have one of those moments of instant mom inspiration that allowed me to magically come up with the perfect response. "Well of course not, sweetie. Those faces are drawn by very talented artists, and they are really pretty and so nicely made, but think about it... Who created *your* face?" She immediately said "Oh, yeah. God." And she grinned with pride. We talked together about how God's work is clearly better than what humans have made, so she is obviously far prettier than a pretend character. And of course we chatted about her other features that cannot be seen, but are far more important.

As I reflected on my response, and wondered how I came up with it so quickly, I realized that this is true in so many different ways. Humans have tried for ages to replicate the beauty of natural Cararra marble. We've tried to make replacements for wood out of vinyl, ceramic, paper, and plastics. We've tried to come up with chemical compounds that can compete with nature's foods, remedies for sunburn that soothe as well as aloe, and fake candles with artificial fire that tries to wiggle just like flames.

Although synthetic plants are starting to look closer to the real thing, and some laminate countertops look like real granite from afar, we've found time and again that it's very difficult to beat nature. Some things cannot be replicated.

In this issue, we're talking about natural materials, natural consequences, natural lessons, natural classrooms, natural scents, and more. In so many cases, what nature has already provided is truly the best solution. We want to apply this philosophy at home, at school, and in our daily routines.

So many trends are leading us away from natural design, including the push for ipads over paper, artificial eyelashes, foods loaded with toxins, and plenty of disposable plastic materials. We want to challenge all that.

Among other mindset shifts, we are also challenging teachers to embrace their natural faces. Skip the makeup and join us for our #naturalteacherface journey, at whatever pace is best for you. See why we're passionate about this on page 20. What I told my daughter was truth. The face you've already got is the true beauty. We want to encourage you to find your confidence by refusing to cover it up with human-made beauty items. Don't hide your freckles; love them and show them off! Don't cover the laugh lines that wrinkle around your eyes to show your cheery disposition and make you feel approachable to students; wear them with pride!

After all, you wouldn't cover a gorgeous granite or marble countertop with a laminate that had fewer natural "flaws," would you?

Let Snowday be your guide to a productive, thoughtful, passionate life as an educator AND as a creative, vibrant human soul!

- Brigid

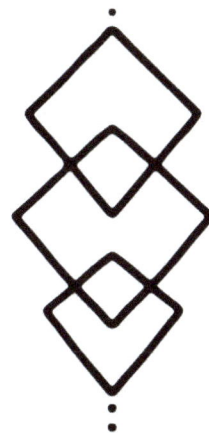

See why we're passionate about this on page 20.

gratitude * health * creativity * spirituality * productivity * beauty * nature * generosity * family * ethics * inspiration

SPOTLIGHT THEME IN THIS ISSUE:
"ALL THINGS NATURAL"

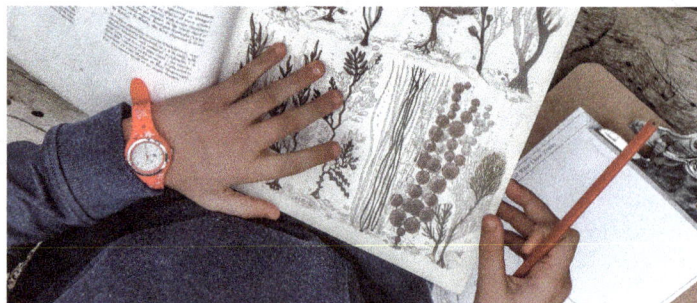

NATURAL INSPIRATION

Human beings need to be outside in nature. The more frequently we're exposed to the outdoors, the healthier and happier we are. We want you and your students to feel the textures of nature and enjoy the smells, sounds, and sights of the outside world even when you are indoors.

NATURAL LEARNING

Lessons that use natural materials and invite exploration have extensive benefits. We're adapting concepts of Reggio-inspired learning to other grade levels and thinking in new ways, plus sharing ideas for natural classrooms, natural lessons, and natural consequences.

NATURAL SELF

Get back to the basics with our natural inspiration for your own body and soul. You'll love the impact of shifting to ingredients found in nature, and our challenge to embrace your natural face, body, and hair!

NATURAL HOME

Natural materials make a home or classroom gorgeous and cozy at the same time. We're featuring a few affordable ways to enjoy a small dose of nature's beauty within your own home and sprinkled throughout your everyday life.

Creativity thrives in quiet, in transition, and in nature.

Objective:
Create a classroom nature corner that fits your students' specific needs.

1. ASSESS:
Do your students need more sensory input and tactile experiences? Or are they in a phase of life where they need to feel they have an "escape?" Do they crave peace in their busy day, and a chance to just reset?

2. PLAN:
Select a corner of the room, preferably by a window with plenty of natural light. Set up seating that will suit your students' needs. Select a time of day for them to access the area, or decide that it will be by their own choice.

3. GATHER:
Seek out natural materials. Students can help with this. For older students, this may mean a succulent garden, a nature sound machine, an essential oil diffuser, and sand to rake or stones to stack. For younger kids, it may be a collection of pinecones to break apart, flowers to arrange, wooden branch slices to stack and line up, herbs to smell, or animal books to explore.

4. TEACH:
Show students how you expect them to take care of this area. Define clearly what they should do to keep it clean, and how they can participate by bringing items or enjoying those that are there.

It turns out that time spent in nature decreases stress hormone levels, strengthens the immune system, lowers blood pressure, fights depression, and improves mental health in both adults and children.

Shinrin-yoku

Numerous studies have resulted in positive findings of nature's impact on people of all ages. In Japan, experts studied the physiological effects of Shinrin-yoku, taking in the forest atmosphere. Shinrin-yoku experts share that "It was developed in Japan during the 1980s and has become a cornerstone of preventive health care and healing in Japanese medicine. Researchers primarily in Japan and South Korea have established a robust body of scientific literature on the health benefits of spending time under the canopy of a living forest."

The researchers discovered that exposure to nature promotes lower concentrations of cortisol (stress hormone), lower pulse rate and blood pressure, and improved nervous system and immune system functioning than we experience in city environments. Time spent in the earth's natural environment does more than just decrease stress in adults. Children benefit from the influence of nature as well.

Researchers are also now linking time spent in nature with mental health and realizing how profound this connection is. At any age, spending just 20 minutes a day outside can give you an immediate mood boost as well as long-term health benefits.

Even just listening to the sounds of nature can ease anxiety and depression. Studies have shown that whether it's by bringing the nature inside, or going out to be in it, you can battle mental and physical ailments by surrounding yourself with some form of nature.

When you cannot get to the beach, try a sand garden. If you're unable to hike a wooded trail until the weekend, try scenting your home or classroom with pine and listening to a forest audioclip. But then, when the evening or weekend does roll around, get a break from your urban or suburban surroundings, and get outside.

Go kayaking or take a run on a hilly trail. Step over roots and touch tree trunks. Enjoy just sitting still on a fallen log beside a peaceful pond or trickling stream. Go on a hunt to find

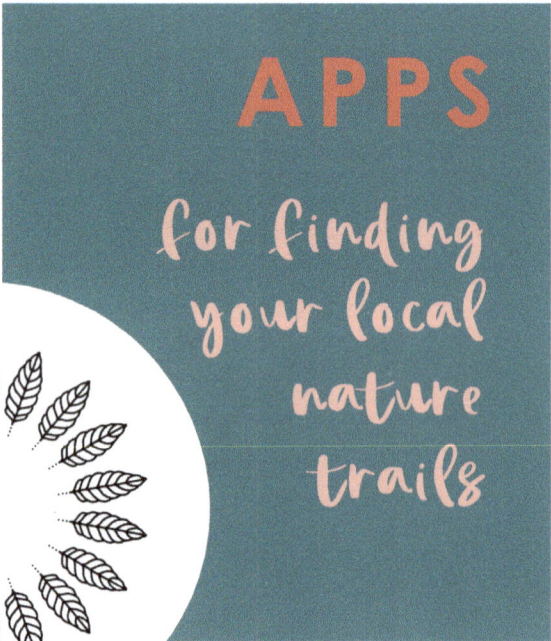

APPS
for finding your local nature trails

VIEWRANGER
Download maps that you can access during an offline hike and discover trail guides.

THE OUTBOUND
Find an adventure wherever you're headed, or right in your own hometown.

KOMOOT
Get a guided plan for your hiking or cycling adventure, even if you are biking in the mountains. Customize your trail based on smoothness of surfaces, level of difficulty, or elevation of the terrain.

the closest waterfall to your home, whether it's small or impressively large.

It's time to get inspired by nature, spend time in nature, and incorporate nature throughout each environment you experience in a day. Prioritize this as self care and to benefit your students. They'll end up focusing and learning more easily, and you may play a small part in helping them avoid anxiety, high blood pressure, and depression in the long run.

natural INSPIRATION

DO
go chasing
waterfalls

Sources: Harvard Health, NaturalLearning.org, NCBI

NATURE'S
powerful effect

scavenger hunt

our nature checklist

➤➤➤

Color as you do / find each one.

🏔 mountain

🌱 farm

⛰ cave

🛶 river

🔥 bonfire

🫐 orchard

📍 island

🌲 forest hike

In addition to physiological benefits, nature has also been found to have a profound effect on our mental health. A study by a team of researchers in Denmark used an extensive personal identification system, which is common in Nordic countries, to provide data for 1 million young adults. The system told researchers essentially everything they needed to know, including their health, needs, and use of public services. They generated a comprehensive and impactful observational study of mental health and the environment.

The team combined long-term data on mental disorder diagnoses from the Danish Psychiatric Central Research Register with years of data taken from satellite imagery that told them about the land.

They adjusted findings to ensure wealth wasn't a factor, and eventually discovered that children raised in the neighborhoods with the least amount of green spaces were 55 percent more likely to develop a mental illness than their peers who grew up in the greenest neighborhoods, regardless of social standing, the area's level of affluence, or parental history of mental illness.

Other recent studies have found compelling evidence of nature's lasting effects on our mind and body. Harvard Health found in 2015 that brains had decreased activity in the prefrontal cortex after walking 90 minutes in nature. This region of the brain focuses on repetitive cycles of negative emotion.

No one knows exactly how nature relaxes us, but we know that it does, and that it's important to keep in mind in educational settings. Our kids need us to prioritize their physical and mental health. If just a few minutes a day spent outside will lead them even slightly toward a mental health boost and away from stress and depression, it's worth it.

You, your family, and your students can all benefit from the impact of interaction with nature. Take this opportunity to brainstorm how you can increase your daily dose of nature at work, at home, and on weekends.

<<<   for your family

for your classroom   >>>

Bring Natural Elements
Into Your Classroom
based on the five senses

Taking your class outside isn't always convenient, or even possible. So, here are some ways you can reap the benefits of nature without actually going outside:

Sight: Upcycle branches and tree trunks for classroom decor. Type this into Pinterest, and you'll get a ton of ideas to create some unique earthy decor. Fasten some wood coins on twine to build natural wooden garland to drape on your walls, or build a natural wood clock with a slab of a tree trunk and some supplies from a craft store.

Sound: Play "Nature Sounds" playlists while your students work. Take a break from music or silence, and search nature sounds on your favorite music-playing platform. You'll be surprised at the benefits of bringing in nature through the sense of sound. Embrace variety by switching between birds, bubbling rivers, storms, and rainforests.

Touch: Rocks, branches and fallen trees can be used for more than just natural decorations. You can use these materials even more purposefully by creating items your students will touch over and over again. Try transforming natural items like pinecones, pebbles, or wood slices into manipulatives, building blocks, or letter magnets. If you discover a fallen tree large enough, you can even make tree trunk stools.

Smell: Diffusing essential oils in your classroom has many benefits, and there are plenty with woodsy or earthy aromas. Try something like Sandalwood, Carrot Seed, or Vetiver to enhance your natural atmosphere. Always double check to make sure essential oils you diffuse in your classroom are 100% safe for kids.

Taste: A special way to incorporate nature through the sense of taste, is to create and nourish your own classroom herb garden. Once the herbs are fully grown, you can let your students pick them, sniff them, and taste them. All you need is a nice windowsill that gets some sunlight. Choose a few potted herbs, like basil, mint, and sage.

Try growing a classroom pizza garden. It will incorporate most of the senses and offer an immersive experience with nature. Students can plant basil, oregano, tomatoes, and even toppings such as peppers and chives. Everyone will enjoy the bounty when you have a fun pizza party using the home-grown ingredients that the students maintained with care for the whole season.

natural CLASSROOMS

Jerrica Lee, an educational consultant for the *Wildflower Collective* uses plain, dry oats as a solid sensory fill. Natural wood containers and scoops offer plenty of options, and a tree section makes a perfect tray.

@raisewildflowers

WHY SHOULD NATURE BE INCLUDED IN EDUCATION?

There are plenty of reasons to take your class to natural settings, or bring natural elements into your classroom, including physical, mental, social, and even relaxation benefits for children and teens.

The *Natural Learning Initiative* is an organization that was founded in 2000 with the purpose of promoting the importance of the natural environment in the daily experience of all children, through environmental design, action research, education, and dissemination of information. They provide a ton of great resources for the why and the how of nature in education. (naturallearning.org)

It's clear that nature promotes a healthy learning environment. The director of NLI, Robin C. Moore, states in an article, "Natural settings stimulate all aspects and stages of child development through multi-sensory experience. They integrate informal play with formal learning in natural learning cycles and thus help build the cognitive constructs necessary for sustained intellectual development."

The artificial turf @littlepeople_learning laid in her reading area is actually a rug from Ikea. The lattices are attached with simple adhesive hooks to keep them in place. She used plants and other natural textures to round out the outdoor feel.

Students Make *Potion Recipes* with a Cross-Curricular Nature Experience

"This particular set up followed on from the children's interests surrounding nature and also unicorns. They had an initial interest in nature after several activities linked to *The Gruffalo*. Then one of the children brought in a story called *How to Catch a Unicorn*. We had set a trap in the classroom to catch the unicorn and the next day received a letter with some ideas - one of them being 'petal potions.'

This invitation to learn linked to different areas of the EYFS curriculum. The children used lots of communication and language to describe and discuss. They talked about the different leaves and flowers and their similarities/differences therefore linking to their understanding of the world. They used fine motor skills to cut, separate, tear apart and crush the different flowers or leaves. They counted petals and measured liquids linking to Maths and also wrote their own recipes linking to Literacy. All of this whilst being creative and using their imagination linking back to the unicorn story. *Truly magical!* "

@awe_and_wonderful

@littlepeople_learning uses plenty of natural materials in her "Invitation to Learn" areas in her classroom in Hunter Valley, Australia.

Process Art with *Nature Paint Brushes*

@awe_and_wonderful also offers the idea of engaging students by "exploring the different textures and creating different patterns with nature paint brushes." She had her students learn about mixing paint colors while incorporating descriptive language, patterns, and natural textures in class.

note taking
DIGITAL VS. BY HAND

With one school after another "going digital," it's more important than ever to resist the paperless trend that has arisen in education. Technology integrations make so many things possible that were not options before, like manipulating geometry software to see 3d models, having customized student-centered apps, and trying virtual learning. These opportunities must not be passed up, and schools have jumped on board to take advantage of all the benefits of their new devices. But administrators, teachers, and students must be cautioned not to eliminate paper and pencil activities altogether.

With one-to-one device to student ratios becoming more common, it seems to be an obvious solution to just have each student keep all notes, texbooks, and schoolwork in a digital format on the device. Excitedly, the administration cuts copy machine limits way back and nearly eliminates all paper from the building.

Great for the environment, not so great for student learning. We need to re-evaluate our true priorities in education. If retention, deep understanding, and student learning are at the forefront, the recent research about digital learning must be taken into account.

The connections the brain makes when the hands are writing is stronger than it is with technology. This can be seen in a study published in *Psychological Science* by Pam Mueller & Daniel Oppenheimer of Princeton University and UCLA. Several students wrote out their notes either by hand or on a laptop. The study found that the students that wrote their notes by hand actually learned more. Their memory was tested for factual detail, conceptual comprehension, and synthesizing capabilities.

While the students who used laptops ended up with more words from the lecture in their notes, their understanding of the concepts were weaker than the students that hand wrote their notes.

This study is actually a great illustration of Robert A. Bjork's 20 year old concept, "desirable difficulty." It simply states that sometimes,

doing things the easy way actually hinders our ability to learn. Obstacles that frustrate us help us learn. While technology can make note taking and learning seem easier and more fun, it takes away the challenge and creativity.

One of the main challenges in handwriting notes is discerning what information to take down. A method like visual note taking is another way to help students retain information. Students can feel empowered when taking down notes by hand. They are in charge of the information they are learning as well as how it is presented on their notes, taking them to another level of engagement in the lesson.

Another key feature of note taking on paper is the hand's participation. Particularly with interactive notes, the hands must engage more fully than they do while typing on a keyboard. The hand to mind connection allows the neurons to ignite. Busy hands involved in a process have been shown to activate the brain and offer bonus rewards as well, such as stress relief.

To maximize these benefits, try visual note taking, which also integrates both brain hemispheres and takes advantage of Dual Coding Theory to strengthen focus and memory. When you can integrate sketches and visual input alongside the linguistic input of the lecture, the brain pathways light up and students remember lesson material better.

It would be a disservice to our students to eliminate all technology from the classroom. After all, this is the 21st century. Having tech skills is a necessity for success in the workforce. That's why we do need to incorporate iPads, laptops, and apps. It is important that students understand the place technology has in the world.

The technology in the classroom must be used in harmony with paper - pencil and hands on strategies. When your devices enhance your lesson, embrace them. Just be aware that math practice, writing work, and notes have to continue to take place on paper in order to allow for the strongest levels of brain processing.

LETTING STUDENTS TAKE NOTES ON A TABLET OR LAPTOP MAY BE IMPEDING THEIR ABILITY TO PROCESS, RECALL, AND RETAIN THE MATERIAL.

Three Ways TO AMP UP NOTETAKING

Visual Interactive Doodle Notes®

take advantage of brain processing to help students focus, relax, and remember. This strategy incorporates memory triggers and interactive tasks that activate neural pathways that lead to retention. Learn more about this method and access free templates and resources at doodlenotes.org.

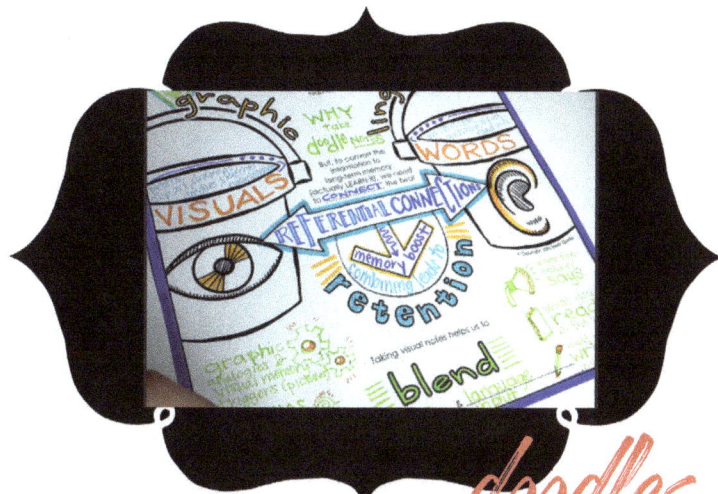

doodles

Notebook Stickers

can help students organize a page based on the structure of a lesson. Just print a basic graphic organizer on full page sticker sheets, or try printing smaller elements on label paper. Students can then make any page instantly come alive with the background flowchart, web, or organizer that they need to fill in or embellish.

stickers

Bite Sized Organizer Cards

offer a more manageable way to review, take notes, or create a study guide. This deck of 100 can be used in many different ways in any classroom. When using graphic organizers, be sure to offer plenty of layouts so students can customize the structure for any type of lesson content.

cards

Image credit, resources, and more information available: **mathgiraffe.com**

YOUR GUIDE TO WOOD TYPES

cedar

Cedar is lightweight and water resistant, so it is often used outdoors, especially in shingles and fences. The wood from this evergreen is known for its wonderful scent, which is why so many people like to use it in a closet or blanket chest, where the clothing will absorb the woody smell. It also resists insects. Try using cedar wood for building an outdoor planter or bench. You'll be able to lift it easily, and it will weather to a silvery hue. If you prefer the natural wood tone coloring, you can prevent silvering by oiling it.

maple

Maple comes in several varieties, including hard, soft, spalted, quilted, curly, and birdseye, among others. It is a dense hardwood that is light in color. Maple is used in contemporary furniture and is a popular choice for tables, cutting boards, and baseball bats. Since maple has a closed grain, it will not take stain well, so it's best with a natural finish. To complement your maple, try a contrasting accent in walnut or cherry. Maple floors and furnishings bring a cozy, bright Scandinavian vibe to a home.

white oak

White oak is an American hardwood that has long been a staple in Craftsman and Mission style furniture. However, it is now making a comeback in some contemporary furniture. It is a dense hardwood with an open grain. It takes stain well but also looks great with a natural finish. White oak can be found quartersawn, rift sawn, or flat sawn. Quartersawn is famous for having its beautiful medullary rays exposed. Due to the density of the wood, white oak can even be suitable for some outdoor uses.

poplar

Poplar is low cost and easy to paint. You will have no trouble finding this species of wood at your local home center. Use it for simple projects, like making a picture frame, trim, wall paneling, or any other crafty DIY you want to tackle. Left natural, poplar can have a greenish or purple hue that is not generally as attractive as some other woods, but it's a great choice for a project that will end up being painted.

walnut

Walnut is an American hardwood that has been made popular along with the new trend of live-edge furniture, where a slab of the tree is cut in a way that preserves the contours of the natural edge. It's considered by many to be the most beautiful of the domestic hardwoods. Its rich, brown color pairs well with a lighter wood like maple. Consider a clear finish that will highlight the natural beauty of the wood. Walnut is gaining traction in recent furniture trends, from dining tables to kitchen cabinets.

DIY project coming up? Or are you just trying to figure out which shelf to buy? Select just the right type of wood to use in each home or classroom situation based on the natural features of each species.

The maple dovetail corners on this live-edge end table accent the darker tone of the walnut. The maple doors have a natural finish, while the poplar wall paneling is painted to take advantage of the natural pros and cons of each type of wood.

>> Cut a slice off the end of your Christmas tree trunk each year before you put it in water. Use a woodburner to engrave the year, and drill a small hole through it for a ribbon or string. You can eventually have a tree filled with natural ornaments that are also a memento of each year's tree.

>> Use a few strands of twinkle lights and a small stack of old firewood to make a "fireplace" or "campfire" in your classroom. Sit around it for special events, like debates, review games, songs, or reading time. It will offer a sense of peace and community, just like when you sit around the fire at home.

>> Scraps of leftover maple or walnut can be used to create a handsome, yet durable cutting board. A little wood glue and a lot of sanding will do the trick to bring it together. This is an easier project than you may guess, and makes a great gift. YouTube videos can help if you are not sure how to glue wood together. Finish with mineral oil or another food safe cutting board application. Scientists are now even finding that wood has natural antibacterial properties! Never put a wooden cutting board in the dishwasher.

>> If you like the look and feel of bare wood, consider a natural oil finish to bring out the grain and color. The oil offers a more pleasing, tactile finish than a poly, which puts a film on top of the wood.

Ideas

FACES

natural

you may be surprised at the feeling of empowerment you can acheive by learning to enjoy the beauty of your natural face

Do you wear cosmetics as armor? Do you feel less secure and unprepared to face a day without it? Biologically, makeup can interfere with the cells' natural renewal processes, but on an emotional level, it can also have long-term impact on your confidence and stress levels.

Your skin is the largest organ in your body. You are probably already aware that any toxins or chemicals in the products that you put on your face can get absorbed into the bloodstream. But did you know that your makeup may also be causing your acne, has potential to give you headaches, and can lead to a cycle of lower self-confidence in some women?

We want to encourage you to embrace your natural face! Yes, this can seem like a daunting challenge. But before you rule out the option of ditching or decreasing your cosmetics, note that even going one day a week without makeup can minimize your pores, boost your body image over time, and give your skin a healthier glow. If you give it long enough, you'll even find some other surprising effects along the way.

Some women have headaches, acne, or anxiety that they never realized may be linked to their cosmetics habits.

Is makeup your adult security blanket?

exterior beauty truly is all about the sparkle in your eyes and the smile on your face

bonus points

>> You'll save time getting ready in the morning. Imagine what you could do with those 15 minutes. Pray, meditate, eat a healthier breakfast, spend time with your kids or husband, enjoy a quick workout, or even get some planning done!

>> Your budget will be impacted. You will be surprised at what you have been spending on cosmetics. How will you spend that money each month now?? The possibilities are exciting!

>> You'll send a message to your young students that you love the way you look just as you are! Show them that you embrace your natural beauty. If they ask why you have cut back or quit on makeup, tell them that you believe you are beautiful and love having your natural face on display, and that they are each beautiful just the way they are too!

embrace your face

Although stats from 2012 found that many women feel "self conscious," "unattractive," or even "naked" without makeup, and only 3 percent of women in the study reported feeling more beautiful without makeup, there may be reasons to start embracing makeup-free days more often.

Way back in 1982, researchers found that women's own beliefs about themselves often became self-fulfilling prophecies. Wearing makeup in an effort to boost self image led many women to depend more on their makeup after it brought the confidence that led to better social interactions. They felt better, so they got social rewards that subconsciously caused them to connect the makeup with that positive feeling. However, when a woman acheives this confidence without makeup, then the cycle does the opposite and leads her to feel better and more self-assured by continuing to embrace her own skin. The perception of others is in fact directly linked to the woman's perception of herself.

It turns out that women who wear makeup less frequently have higher self esteem and are more emotionally stable. If you'd like to start getting comfortable in your own skin, you may want to tackle this challenge all at once or more gradually. Even if you choose to cut back on cosmetics one step at a time, you can acheive the mental health benefits of baring your natural skin. With the current focus on authenticity, it's a great time to embrace your face!

Share your
#naturalteacherface

look your best

In addition to renewed confidence after quitting makeup completely, here's what a few women have reported:

>> clearer skin - no more breakouts
>> less stress
>> no more headaches (a hidden allergic reaction)
>> younger appearance
>> less defined wrinkles
>> more relaxed mornings
>> no more dry skin
>> fewer eye infections
>> smaller pores
>> beginning to love natural features like freckles

Here's how to look your best without makeup and love the face you wake up with:

Keep hair freshly cut. When your face and hair look healthy and well cared for, you naturally look your best.

Smile! It truly enhances your beauty.

Prioritize sleep. Rather than hiding dark eyes, keep yourself rested and healthy. You'll look *and feel* brighter!

Be confident. Expect to feel beautiful all day and you will. Plus, others perceive you based on how you hold yourself.

Skincare Tips for Going Natural

Exfoliate

Using a facial scub twice a week helps remove or minimize any acne, scars, or blemishes. Exfoliating also reveals fresh, healthier, smoother skin.

Hydrate

Keep skin moisturized by drinking plenty of water and by using a healthy moisturizer each day, preferably one with sunscreen.

Supplement

Vitamins like E, C, and K are great skin boosters. Avoid overexposing yourself to sunshine, but try to soak up at least 10-15 minutes of Vitamin D each day too.

Healthy fats are another great solution. They'll give your skin a healthy glow. Try nuts, seeds, avocado, and plenty of fish.

Wait

After a few weeks, your pores may reward you for letting them breathe. Many women notice a decrease in acne and slowly get used to makeup-free living. Give it time. If you throw in the towel too soon, you may not have noticed all the physical and emotional benefits yet. Give your face and your mind both time to adjust.

Look in the mirror each day and take a moment to reflect on the aspects of your natural face that you love. Enjoy whatever journey you choose to embrace your face in your own way!

Take a moment to reflect...

When you assess your relationship with makeup, do so based on how you feel WITHOUT it.

For you, is makeup armor? Does it make you feel protected and ready for the day?

Or in your case is it more like a security blanket? Do you feel comforted by your cosmetics once they are applied?

Is it more of a hobby to you? Or perhaps it is simply something you connect with a routine? Do you wear makeup for date night, but not for school each day?

Take time to evaluate how you use makeup and how you feel both with and **without** it. Reading this may make you want to defend your own makeup habits. And they may be perfectly healthy! Just ensure that you reflect on your relationship with makeup based on how you honestly feel without it to find your own truth. It's different for everyone. Are you perfectly content with your habits, or is it time to make a bold shift?

"Art for me is my ministry. I believe that God has gifted creatives with the ability to emphasize the beauty He has already displayed around us."

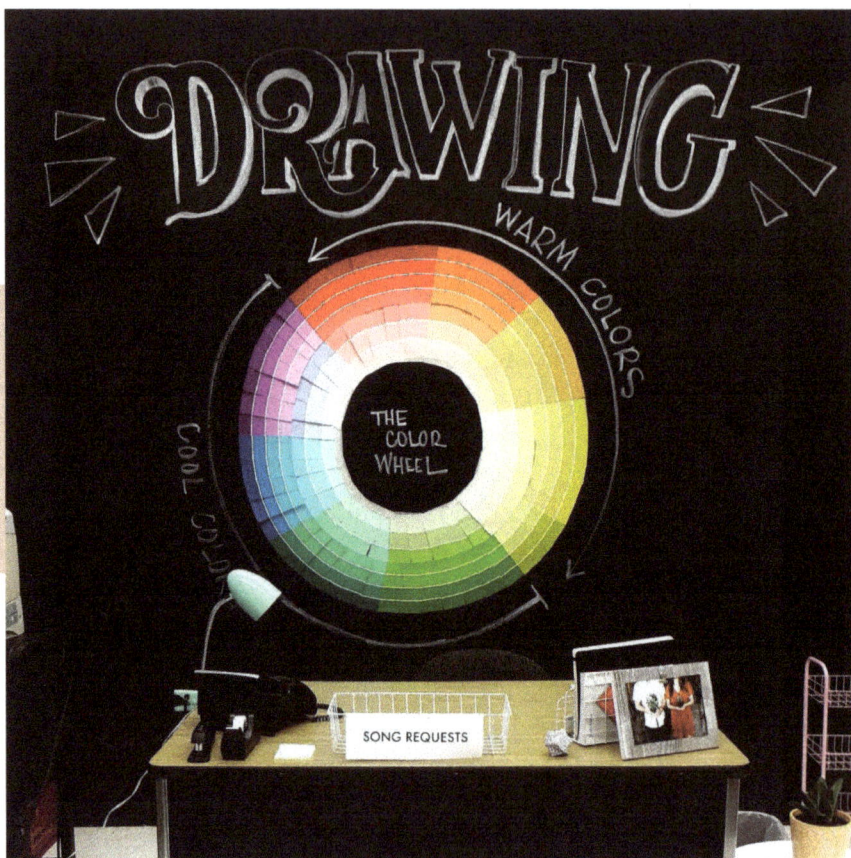

Kristen Yann
@KRISTENYANNART

>> painter
>> teacher
>> follower of Christ

I have been painting and drawing for as long as I can remember. Even at the age of 5 years old, I knew I wanted to be an artist when I grew up. After high school, I studied at Florida State University and received my Bachelor's of Fine Arts Degree in Studio Art. My long term goal was to make art and live off of it, as any artist dreams to. Just recently however, I was presented with the opportunity to teach at the very high school I attended myself growing up. It was such a unique and spur of the moment offer, one that I hadn't even applied for, so I decided to give teaching a shot. So far, it has stretched me in ways no other job has (teaching art and making art are two completely different things). Nonetheless, I am thankful for this experience and the ways that it is shaping me already.

Life as an Artist and Teacher

My work is deeply rooted in my faith. I believe that I was gifted by God with an innately creative spirit my entire life. Art never was just an interest to me. It was, and is, as natural as breathing in my life. In Kindergarten, I had a teacher that looked at a drawing I had done of an astronaut and proclaimed, "Kristen, you are going to be an artist someday!".

It was as if she put a label to what I had already known I wanted to do forever, even at just five years old. Once I knew the official title of my intrinsic desire, painting and sketching and all other forms of expression just fueled my pursuit.

I live in a little town in Central Florida. It's one of those small towns you see in the movies, you know, where everyone knows everyone. Growing up in a small town had its ups and downs, but it is a particularly challenging environment as an educator. The funds are lacking, and the appreciation for the arts and humanities take little precedence over sports and agricultural programs.

My environment is extremely impactful on my emotional state, which is why my classroom and home environments are usually beaming with creative elements. Currently, I am working from home and/or my classroom. My dream is to

eventually have a studio away from home, but until then, I make do with what is available!

Work Transitions Over Time

My work started out primarily as traditional figurative work. However, after a tragic encounter with a passed love one, my personal experience was able to shape my art conceptually and bring a deeper meaning into my art. While my art still remains figurative, there has been a shift in narrative and even in style.

Fueling the Soul

My favorite spot to fuel my soul is in the woods. Hiking, camping, running... it doesn't matter to me. There is something magical that happens when we allow ourselves to be immersed in nature, and I think there's something to be said for that.

Art for me is my ministry. I believe that God has gifted creatives with the ability to emphasize the beauty He has already displayed around us. I prioritize my creative passion because as an artist, I am able to bring glory to the master creator Himself.

The Art Classroom

My favorite area of my classroom is my chalk wall! When I first was hired as an art teacher for PHS, I was given an old science room that was far from being a creative space. Our fire code limits us when it comes to classroom décor because only 20 percent of our walls are technically allowed to be covered with any form of paper decoration.

After a while considering a way around this, I decided to paint an entire wall with flat black paint and fill it with chalk drawings.

By doing so, I was not only able to spruce up the space in a creative way, but I was able to without breaking any fire code rules! It was definitely a win/win, and my students LOVE it! They draw on it just about every day.

Paint Tip >>

If working with oil paint, a pro tip is to store your palette in the freezer when you're done. This way, your paint will not oxidize quickly and it will be fresh for use the next day!

I prioritize my creative passion because as an artist, I am able to bring glory to the master creator Himself.

See Kristen's own art on Instagram: @kristenyannart

There is something magical that happens when we allow ourselves to be immersed in nature

The educators in my district struggle with closing the learning gap (we serve mostly minority groups), while keeping learning interesting and fun. It is so hard to have urgency and engagement at the same time!

>> Teresa,
Secondary Math and CTE

My biggest challenge as an educator is the increasing number of students who lack intrinsic motivation and personal accountability. I believe this is often fueled by constantly offering incentives to students to make right choices without consequences and accountability for poor choices. Administrators love PBIS, but in my opinion it does not do the job of building character in the long run.

>> Valerie, First Grade

My current frustration is Admin. acting like our new curriculum is awesome because it's scripted and gives us all the activities we need, and .... free!! But they aren't looking at the quality of it and noticing all the important pieces lacking in it (metacognition, learner preferences, etc.) so we are stuck in a curriculum that's saving the district lots of money but making poor decisions for our kids.

>> Emily, Secondary Mathematics

Discipline in the classroom is the toughest issue. Many of the responses fall into two categories: either "start the year right" kind of suggestions or "motivate your kids" kind of suggestions. I teach in a high school where the kids don't care, are far behind, and do not have a lot of academic support. Many things do not motivate them and detentions, etc. don't correct them.

>> Todd, Instructional Coach

I'm dealing with the lack of support for student behavior issues and ineffective administrators.

>> Lydia, Secondary Social Studies

PASSING

The roots of education are bitter, but the fruit is sweet. >> Aristotle

The biggest challenge facing me right now is trying to prepare my special education students, whose instruction must be differentiated according to the law, to successfully complete a standardized state test in order to graduate.

>> *Ellen,*
High School Special Education

My biggest frustration is that math books are too expensive for my students, and open source books are poor quality.

>> *Judy, Community College Statistics*

My struggle is the pressure to teach to the state assessments rather than teaching for conceptual understanding in all subjects.

>> *Sara, Home Hospital Teacher:*
All Subjects and Grades

I work in a District/Region that does not have art classes for secondary students. I realize that this is not as important as space or staffing. But I find it very frustrating that our region does not regard the arts as an essential experience for our students. Many of our students ask for art classes, especially those who don't fit in with the sports crowd or in band. I don't think our district sees a link between the problem solving skills and the ability to create something by hand. As I scroll down through Instagram, I see so many people that have benefited from being creative and are now business owners that are prospering from their own creativity. As teachers, we do not expose students to this enough. Being happy is all about doing something you love, creating things for others, and putting smiles on other people's faces through our own creation. I am a former art teacher, who moved to math and sciences when I realized there were no jobs in my profession. I love teaching math and science and I do what I can to incorporate creativity in these subjects. But what I do does not compare to the joy of teaching art and the enthusiasm students have for art class. Students are losing interest in school because there is nothing to look forward to. Sure, students may enjoy doing well in a specific test or project. But nothing compares to the sense of accomplishment they feel when they have created something from their soul, and recognizing that hard work and dedication can be accomplished while doing something you love.

>> *Alexandra, Secondary Math & Science*

I would consider the biggest frustration to be lack of space for staff and students. I am a part of our district's alternative high school, and currently we have no building of our own and are housed above the district office. We are quickly growing beyond our walls, but we have nowhere to go. As it stands currently, there are 5 teachers and 3.75 classrooms. (The .75 is the student services "classroom" that has 1 table and can seat 2 students comfortably).

>> *Stephanie, Secondary Mathematics*

What is the biggest challenge facing educators in your area?

NOTES

adapting
Reggio-Inspired
learning

The Reggio Emilia approach to early childhood education views children as unique individuals who are curious about their world and have the powerful potential to learn from all that surrounds them. Reggio teachers apply various strategies in the classroom, such as exposing children to a wide variety of educational opportunities that encourage self-expression, communication, logical thinking, and problem-solving.

After World War II, this educational philosophy was founded by an early childhood educator, Loris Malaguzzi, in Reggio Emilia, Italy. In America and the rest of the world, the correct term is "Reggio-Inspired approach", because the teachers in Reggio Emilia are the only ones who technically use the Reggio approach.

The Reggio-inspired approach is largely shaped by some fundamental principles, including their image of the child, emergent curriculum, in-depth research projects, and collaboration.

by Kelly Barendt

Principles

Image of the Child: With a Reggio-inspired approach, children are viewed as competent, curious, full of knowledge and potential, and interested in connecting to the world around them. Teachers are deeply aware of each child's potential and construct all of their work and the environment the children will experience to respond appropriately. Children have 100 languages (many ways they express themselves). We need to engage all senses.

Emergent Curriculum: A classroom's curriculum stems from the particular interests of children. Curriculum topics are derived from talking with children and their families, as well as from things that are known to be interesting to children (puddles, dinosaurs, and so on). Teachers compare notes and observations in team planning sessions to decide which projects would be best suited to children in their classes, what materials will be needed, and how they can encourage parents and the community to become involved.

In-Depth Projects: These projects are thorough studies of concepts and ideas based on the information gathered about children's interests. Projects are often introduced to children as adventures, and can last anywhere from a week or two to the entire school year. Teachers act as advisors on these projects, helping children decide in which direction they would like to take their research, how they can represent what they learn, and what materials would be best suited for their representations.

Collaboration: The approach values communication, with an emphasis on listening and collaboration.

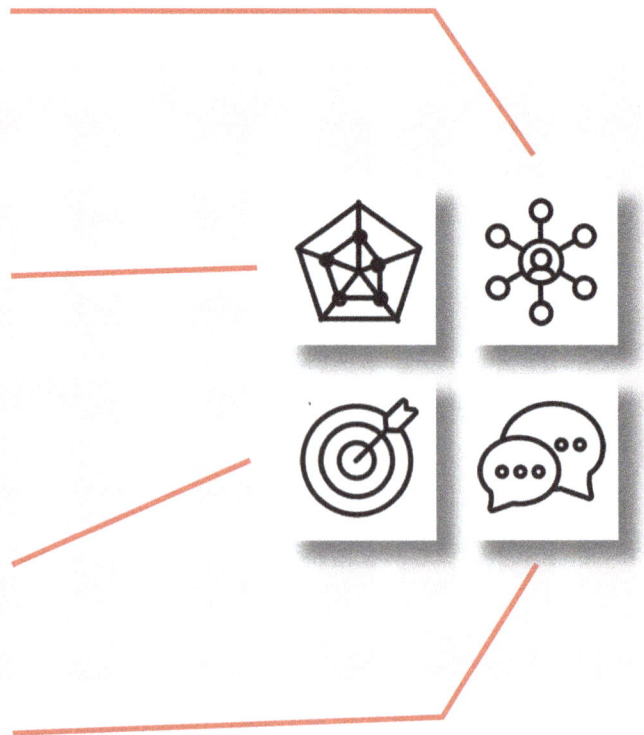

Key Roles in Learning

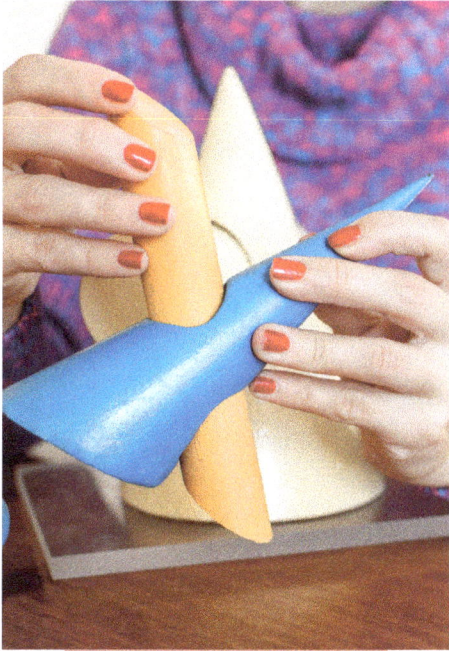

Teacher

Guide, facilitator, and listener.

Knows the end destination, and works alongside the children

Student

Explorer of the environment

Sets the path of learning depending on what they need

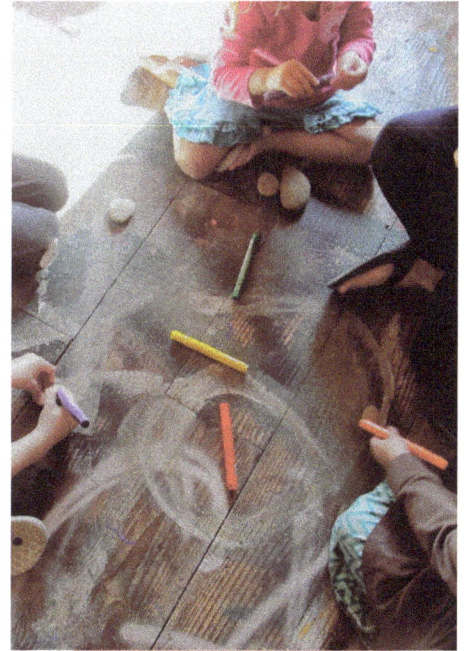

Environment

"The third teacher"

Gives students the tools that they need and stimulates them

Nature and Provocations

Bringing nature into the classroom is a big part of the approach, because it draws students in; it's engaging. A big term in the Reggio-inspired approach is "provocations". Provocations are when teachers leave out interesting materials before a lesson to invite creativity and wonderment. When students enter the classroom, they are immediately drawn to the exciting collection left out for them!

How can we apply this in middle and high school?

To implement the approach with older students, you should start by thinking about the environment. Shift your mindset so that you remember the classroom is not just for you, but can and should inspire your students. For example, the concept of "provocations" applies to any grade level. Have bowls with different supplies (markers, clips, etc.) and poster paper set up around the classroom as the students enter the room. Try setting up an experiment, lab activity, or hands-on inquiry. At any age, human minds get excited to see materials that appear to be intriguing. You can set the stage for investigation. Even just stacks of sticky notes at each group of tables will awaken your students to listen and anticipate what may be coming next. Even as adults, when we walk into a room for professional development, or a staff meeting, we look around and survey the room. We can immediately tell whether this will be something out of the ordinary, or just a typical lecture or boring meeting. If there is something laid out for us in advance, a touch of excitement is already triggered, priming our brains to be more engaged than they would otherwise be.

The principle of involving nature is also easy to implement in upper grades. Can you get students outside to lay pebbles out to form a sine curve? Can you have them search for natural materials outside the school to represent a concept from the lesson? Maybe you can even find ways to bring nature into the room. Just as preschool students arrange loose parts such as stones and slices of branches to model addition and subtraction, your older students can use twigs, shells, and rocks to model types of government, where certain items represent people and others are special "leaders." Or certain loose parts can become positive integers while others become negative to model addition and subtraction with negative numbers. Loose parts can create a mood board representing a novel. They can be used to form hinged creations that represent a simple machine, or the theorems behind congruent triangle shortcuts. Loose parts can be arranged to explore concepts, represent ideas, and encourage hands-on collaboration. The possibilities are endless, so do not feel that the use of tactile, natural items is limited to only the little ones in elementary school. Older kids can benefit from the feeling and sensory input of the textures of the natural world as well. They enjoy getting outside for a mood boost and some fresh air too, and the concept of loose parts forces them to get creative and think outside the room.

In alignment with the Reggio-inspired methods, you can also work to implement more project-based learning in your classes. Let students (with input from parents) select an area of interest to study. Allow some independence blended with appropriate guidance, and have each student investigate topics they enjoy that are connected with learning standards. When incorporating project-based learning, look into concepts like "makerspace" or "genius hour," but be careful to set clear standards and do your research, so no student falls behind. Balance your goals of self-directed inquiry based learning with the needs of teens, and the reality that they will need to accumulate specific skills, coursework, and credits to reach the next steps in their education.

Tips for Getting Started

If you're interested in implementing the Reggio-inspired approach, here are some tips:

Just start; you don't have to have all the answers.

It's important to remember to keep the students' interests in mind and honor their voices, questions, and curiosity.

Collaborate with other teachers. Maybe a fellow teammate is interested in implementing the approach.

Ideas for "Loose Parts"

bottle caps
leaves from herbs
binder clips
nuts and bolts
wood chips
twine or yarn
stones
gravel and jars
acorns
cardboard rolls
springs and hinges
trays
index cards
clamps
hair elastics
scale
seashells
fabric scraps
small branches
clothespins
wooden blocks
sponges
mortar and pestle
small containers
flower parts
velcro strips
cupcake papers
corks
pushpins

Real Talk with RW

Episode 19 "Early Education - The Reggio Emilia Approach"

In this episode, the podcast host interviews her daughter's preschool teacher, who shares her passion for a Reggio-inspired approach.

Teaching Middle School ELA

Episode 9 "Classroom Environment"

Holly from *Research and Play* shares her experience as a kindergarten teacher using the Reggio approach, and offers insights into bringing the approach into middle school classrooms.

Podcast Episodes

The Preschool Podcast

"Reggio Emilia Approach and Pedagogical Documentation"

This episode interviews Diane Kashin, an Early Childhood Education professor at Ryerson University in Toronto. It explores what teachers mean by a Reggio Inspired practice and shares how to implement pedagogical documentation.

inspirED

Episode 2 "Reggio Emilia with Jeni Kersting"

Early Childhood teacher Jeni Kersting shares her passion for and insights on the Reggio Emilia Approach in her pre-K classroom.

The Mud Room

The "Loris Malaguzzi and Reggio Emilia" Episode

This parenting podcast episode dives into the approach, so parents can implement the principles of Reggio-inspired learning with their little ones.

I'm a wife to Matt and mumma to 2 gorgeous little ones, Patrick (4) and Elsie (1). I am the youngest of 5 children. I grew up in a loving Christian family that went camping, fishing, and travelling around Australia often. I'm not afraid to get dirty, I love being spontaneous and adventurous, and my fondest memories with my Dad were spent outdoors. My husband has many of the best qualities that my Dad does and loves camping, adventure, and the outdoors as much as I do. In fact, our first 'date' was finding a wet slippery hill to slide down on a boogie board.

nature based
LESSONS
with natural
MATERIALS

by Liv
@wild.and.play

Natural materials are free, engage all of the senses and provide scope for imagination and creativity through open-ended play. Natural items are also a more sustainable option and better for our environment. Teaching children how to be resourceful with nature is vital in helping the next generations appreciate and care for our planet.

I think ultimately, I am passionate about the wellbeing of children. That's where my priorities in my teaching and as a mum come from. Children these days struggle being bored, are spending more time with technology, and don't get the chance to use their imagination and creativity in a way children once did. Furthermore, research is telling us that our children aren't as happy, healthy, or emotionally resilient. I want to nurture a child's intrinsic curiosity to help them understand themselves and the world around them. I guess in my teaching and parenting, I have found that every child has a universal love for nature. There is not a single child who doesn't love being outdoors in one way or another. There are studies that prove the power of nature having a positive affect on physical health, mental health, and cognitive abilities. So I integrate our natural world in as many ways as I can to make sure these kids are getting the best education AND childhood that they can.

I set up play-based activities for my students that they engage in when they enter the classroom each day. I often make drawing an option. I have many children in my current class that love drawing, so I foster that. Sometimes I give students a physical item to observe and draw, but occasionally I'll give them some illustrations of nature to choose what they wish to draw. Having the nest to look at and touch also helps the children to use their senses to create their picture.

When it comes to resources, don't go out trying to buy/collect/gather a whole heap of natural materials for your class. Be wise. Where you can, create them with your kids and involve them in the process. You'll be surprised at how much collecting sticks and rocks at lunch time thrills some students! The thought of teaching lessons outside can be daunting! I get it. But let go and just take the plunge!

Once you get the hang of it, it is honestly a powerful way to create engaging, relevant and valuable learning experiences. Let the children take the lead at times if you can, and be prepared.

The teacher works with the classroom environment to facilitate optimum and authentic learning. Resources are thoughtfully added, taken away, or displayed to promote creativity, thinking and problem solving skills, questions, experimentation, and open-ended play. Furthermore, the environment of a classroom sets the tone for learning and a place of belonging. My biggest tip is to remove clutter. Focus on open and inviting spaces with natural furnishings that aren't bright and distracting. Present materials and resources to draw attention. Move away from the classroom that looks institutional and more towards one that invites students to explore and create!

HOW DO YOU FIND BALANCE?

Gosh, I wish I had the key to the ultimate balance – but alas, I do not. Teaching is a demanding job and often takes up more time than you're paid for. But my family is my priority, so I make sure I don't have work to bring home. I don't mark at home. I don't have email alerts on my phone. I get to school early and finish a bit later than some teachers so that my days off with the kids are just that – days with my kids (note: I work 2 days a week while my kids are littles).

WHAT FILLS YOUR SOUL?

Jesus. I am unashamedly a lover and follower of Jesus Christ. He fills my soul daily and I find my strength in him. Wine and coffee also fill my soul...I won't lie.

WHAT DO YOU WANT TO TELL THE TEACHERS OF THE WORLD?

You are truly, undoubtedly amazing! That's it. I know how hard this gig can be, I know you are driven by your passion and not by money or fame. I know your heart is golden and your intentions are great. You are amazing.

life soul balance

WOODWORKING, BUILDING, AND USING ADULT TOOLS

Using real tools as opposed to plastic toy tools is a very powerful 'tool' in itself. (See what I did there?) It provides children a way to actively learn in a real-life situation, assess risk, develop independence and responsibility, and feel valued and trusted by the adult initiating the play. I do not discourage the use of pretend tools; there is definitely a place for them too, but allowing children to explore real tools is giving them an opportunity to show that they are capable learners! This also is transferrable to knives and kitchen tools too, not just woodworking and building.

KID ARTWORK HACK

If you don't know what to do with all the hundreds of art pieces your kids give you...turn them into gift cards or wrapping paper!! I am not a hoarder AT ALL and don't like clutter (Don't worry, I keep the really significant drawings!), so I have found a great way to reuse the old drawings is to make cards for our family and friends!

APPLYING THESE STRATEGIES FOR OLDER STUDENTS

We are all individuals with our own interests, our own abilities and our own personalities. Our role as adults is to create an environment where children can shine regardless of who they are. This doesn't change for older students or teenagers. Even more so with older students, technology is becoming an addiction and an indoor lifestyle is becoming prevalent. Taking lessons outdoors and involving nature in their learning has just as much benefit for these children as it does in the early years.

WHAT ARE YOU MOST GRATEFUL FOR?

My husband. I can't really put into words how grateful I truly am. He is my ultimate soul mate. My best friend. My giving, domesticated, funny, patient, massive hearted MacGyver who lacks in nothing when it comes to resourcefulness and skill. He gave me children, he has taught me how to love others, and he gives the best massages. He does take 1 hour to say goodbye and leave ANY event, but it's only because he genuinely wants to listen to and learn about others. So I'll forgive him....sometimes.

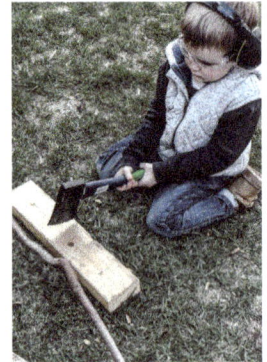

Birds

Bowls

$2

$2

Food

Pet Wash

pet shop play

acidic science experiment

I used red cabbage indicator to make magical potions with acids and bases from around the home. This is such a wonderful activity that we reset and did it twice more.

I'd say it took up a good hour of our day. Patrick could have kept going! It truly is magical. You start with red cabbage and get the natural purple colour from it using boiled water (I was cleaning out the fridge and actually had a jar of red cabbage I was chucking out! It was fate!!)

Find some acids and bases around the home (that are colourless). I used:
• milk
• bicarb
• citric acid
• laundry powder
• sparkly water
• vinegar

As you add some red cabbage liquid to the acids and bases, they change colour! Amazing. It was just as fun for me as it was for Patrick. This is a really cool activity for older kiddos too.

Patrick loves to put everything we ever make or do all together (cringe) so he had a great time adding all the components into one jar. And guess what happened when he finally added the vinegar to the bicarb!? - He made some amazing volcanoes and both times were an amazing surprise because we had no idea what was what!

outdoor math classes

I have embraced nature as the best free resource and I try to get outside as often as possible.

One of my favourite subjects to address outdoors is maths. If you would like to get outside more with your class or child, I would strongly suggest you invest in the book *Messy Maths*. It's jam packed full of ideas for outdoor math lessons in all math topics!

Create an analogue clock with a hoop, rocks, and sticks. During this task, I was able to see which students knew about clocks very clearly. Some had clocks set out like this one. Some added tiny sticks for the minutes scale, some added a seconds hand, some had hands the same size, some had all the numbers but bunched in one side of the clock face. You get the picture.

After they took a photo of their clock, I called out some times to test what they knew about where the hands should be.

I had an analogue clock with me to show them the answer and when it came to manipulating their own designs, many students realised where they made mistakes on their clock face and why they needed to fix it for their clock to run smoothly. Now we have a heap of numbered stones for many other math tasks in the future.

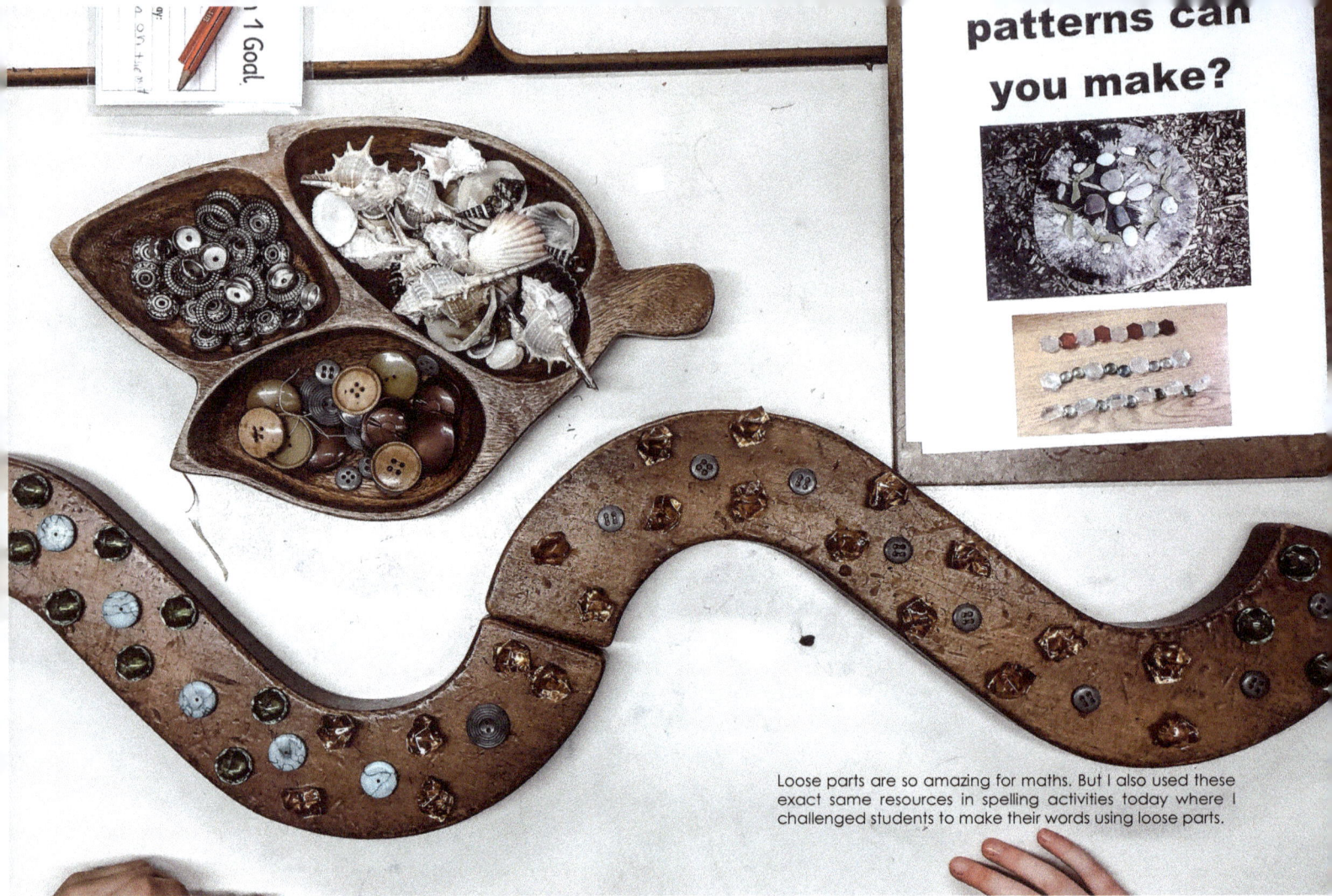

patterns can you make?

Loose parts are so amazing for maths. But I also used these exact same resources in spelling activities today where I challenged students to make their words using loose parts.

"Studies do show that an outdoor lifestyle for children predicts future physical health, future mental health, and future cognitive abilities. We can change it, even if it's one single day of the week that we scrap all devices and dedicate to fun and playing outside, regardless of the weather.

What day will you choose? Whether you are a parent or an educator, pick a day of the week to dedicate to the outdoors. Not just away from devices and tv, but outdoors!

Go. Do it.
And then come back and tell me it didn't do wonders for you and your child."

Follow Liv on Instagram
@wild.and.play

5 TIPS FOR INCLUDING NATURE IN YOUR CLASSROOM:

1. Get students to bring in rain jackets and gumboots for the year, so you can get outdoors no matter the weather.

2. Have a stash of sticks, rocks, shells, and conifers on hand for **so** many different activities.

3. Do a nature walk every day. It can be 5 minutes or it can be an hour. It can have a purpose or it can be completely open to whatever the students like. It can be for relaxation or it can be for burning energy. I've used nature walks for mindfulness, just walking in silence to count how many birds are heard. I've used nature walks to look for insects. I've used nature walks just to jump in puddles at the end of the day! They are all loved by the kids. They are all beneficial.

4. Try to find nature field guides for your area with birds, fungi, flowers, trees, and insects! It is great to have a point of call for when students find something on a nature walk that they are intrigued by.

5. Find a place in the school where your students can create a garden in the soil or in pots! There is something spectacularly educational about growing plants. Watching the process, caring for something, using the product... it is a cross curricula life skill that is great for any age!

Bugs lend themselves to so many wonderful mathematical concepts: symmetry, counting legs in twos, patterns, and fractions (the thirds of their anatomy), to name a few.

A Hand-Sized Scavenger Hunt

Trace your hand here:

Collect these things and tick them

A stick smaller than my hand	A blade of grass longer than my little finger	A leaf as wide as my hand span	A nut the size of my thumbnail
A flower that fits in my palm	A bark chip that fits inside my middle finger	Something as long as my pointer finger	Something as wide as my wrist

Stick or draw your collection on your traced hand above

on the go play kits

A fantastic way to occupy kids in imaginative play when you are travelling or headed out is to create little play kits packed with a range of materials.

I like to include play dough, some characters (bugs, fairies, animals, sea life...whatever theme you like), and then some loose parts.

These can be natural things like sticks, rocks, shells, conifers, or gumnuts, or they can be items like story stones, letters, numbers, or beads. Anything!!

I haven't used them in the classroom yet, just with my 4 year old. But that is a great idea!

These kits would work fantastically for children with sensory needs who may need to cool down, or for quiet time too.

fabric
GIFT WRAP

Fabric wrapping is not a new concept, but if you have not explored the possibilities, it's a great time to begin. Whether your goal is to be more environmentally conscious, or to save money and trips to the store by switching to a more permanent option, this method may be right for you. Centuries ago, tsutsumi (meaning "packaging") was used in Japan, and then later the name for the fabric wraps changed to furoshiki ("bath spread"). At the bathhouse, guests would wrap their kimonos up in different furoshiki designs while they bathed. This helped them find their own clothing afterward and prevented confusion, much like wine glass tags used at parties. Koreans used a similar reusable wrapping cloth called the bojagi, which was usually made of silk. Eventually, the Chinese developed paper, and wrapping presents in paper began.

Now, Americans are consuming 85 million tons of paper each year, and it's estimated that almost half of it is for wrapping paper, packaging, and decoration. We spend around three billion dollars annually on wrapping paper, and it generally goes straight into the trash bin. The anticipation and surprise of a wrapped gift is central to many celebrations, but is it critical that we wrap in such a wasteful way? It may be time to rediscover fabric as a wrapping material that can be used over and over.

When you gift outside of your own family, the fabric adds to the present as well. Friends will enjoy using the cloth to wrap up bento box lunches, create a purse or produce bag for grocery shopping, or re-gift as packaging and pass it on. Try adding decorative accents on top, such as flowers, wooden cooking utensils, or decorative tags.

MAKE YOUR OWN
Try stenciling your own pattern
on plain cloth with fabric paint

Choose one fabric pattern or color for each family member, and re-use them each year. One square yard of fabric works for most gifts, but you can make a few oversized wraps as well for larger presents.

We made ours without any sewing, but if you have a machine and the desire, you can make lined wraps that have an accent color on the reverse.

Tie a loose single knot by twisting the tails together, then gently tie another flat single knot on the underside.

2

1

the "hug twist"

First position the gift diagonally in the center and wrap in one direction. Twist the tails that will wrap in the other direction.

>> SILK
>> COTTON
>> NYLON
>> OLD CLOTH
  NAPKINS
>> BANDANAS

Tie a knot in each corner of the wrap, leaving a long tail in all four corners.

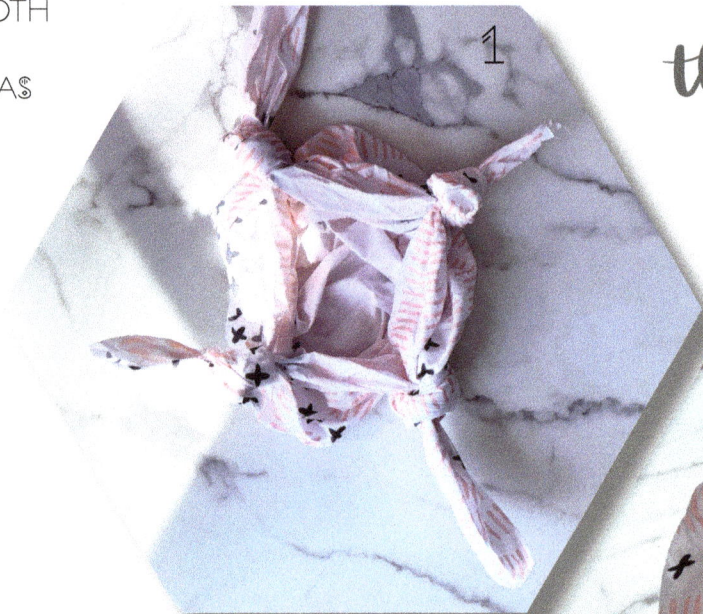

the two handle bag

Take two adjacent tails and knot them together. A loop will form to act as the handle. Take the remaining two tails and do the same to create the second handle.

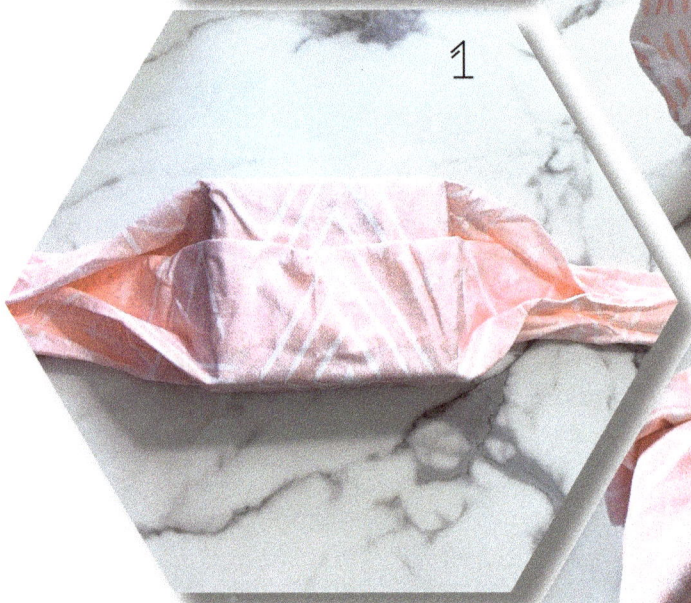

Wrap the package lengthwise, then fold the excess on each side towards the seam lenthwise to make the side flaps narrow.

the simple knot

Tie a single loose knot as shown, wrapping the tails around the corners and fluffing them back out to enclose each corner as shown, or try a double knot and leave the tails on top as a bow instead (previous page, left).

the wine bottle wrap

Place the wine bottle in the lower right hand corner of the cloth. Wrap it, cupping the bottom with the wrapping cloth, but only roll it one complete roll toward the left, then stop. Fold the excess cloth down from the top, then up from the bottom as well to narrow it down. Fold up enough to create an upward angle as shown in picture 2 above. This will form a spiral up the bottle as you roll. As you roll, you can fold again to narrow the tail further. Tuck the final tail in.

Ready to get more crafty with it? Try these hashtags to see fancier options for tying your wraps:

#FUROSHIKI
#REUSABLEGIFTWRAP
#FABRICGIFTWRAP
#BOJAGIWRAPPING

CONSEQUENCES

natural

At some point in every school year you will have to deal with students that break the rules and challenge authority, and it can be difficult to know how to respond. Natural consequences are a heathy way to address negative behaviors in a way that sets students up to understand the direct influence that their actions have.

Instead of being based on pre-created behavior management systems, natural consequences use logic to determine what is appropriate for each unique situation. Approaching behavioral challenges with an attitude of logic helps you stop and think: What type of response could turn the infraction into a teachable moment or into an outlet for resentment?

This is where responsive classroom management comes in. This means that every day lessons include academics as well as social and emotional impacts of individual actions. This type of management or discipline is based around forming and maintaining a respectful relationship. Students develop the skill of thinking ahead to anticipate the natural consequences of their actions.

For some teachers, this will come naturally. But if you have a hard time instantly coming up with just the right natural consequence in the moment, it helps to have examples to set you up for success. Most situations fall into

Natural consequences convey a lesson instead of just doling out punishment. Children and adolescents not only have a chance to see the error in their behavior, but also will see how to fix it. Show your students how their choices affect them and others, and give them a chance to learn and improve their actions in the future.

a few categories. If you know these and practice the responses, you'll get to the point where you can look to just the right type of natural consequence and see the benefits immediately with your class.

Many cases fit into having to fix or undo the effect of a student's poor choice. These would include consequences such as cleaning up trash throughout the school after being caught throwing garbage on the ground. Many other situations will be able to fall into the category of "time," where you show students that if they chat too much, or dilly dally with cleanup, then there is no time left for the privilege or reward they may have wished for.

Once you get a handle on the different varieties of student actions and match them up with the most appropriate and natural consequence, you'll begin to get in the groove and flow into the right reaction right away each time.

In parenting, the idea is that we love our children enough to have strong, consistent expectations and enforce reasonable guidelines. A child who knows what is expected and has clear procedures in place is actually happier. This is beneficial in the classroom as well.

The logic part comes in when we allow kids to learn decision making, benefit from their mistakes in the long run, and experience natural repercussions of their actions. When the logical consequences are balanced with love and empathy, the child grows and is able to learn to make smart choices and live a happy and fulfilled life.

To teach students self-discipline with clear expectations, we can approach classroom management with a simple balance of loving structure and logical repercussions.

Benefits of Loving Structure Blended with Natural Consequences

>> Students who feel respected, and even loved, will be less motivated to intentionally cause discipline problems.

>> Students feel more relaxed when they know that they have a good blend of both choices and reasonable limits.

>> Problem solving and decision making skills are nurtured over time.

>> Misbehavior is actively prevented, removing the need to constantly address it.

>> In cases where consequences are needed, a teacher can effectively guide the student to see the natural repercussions, and learn and grow from the experience.

What About Teens and Pre-Teens?

It's no secret that parents, teachers, and even students are not fans of suspension as a form of punishment. However, it still seems to be one of the most common forms of punishments that schools offer as students get into the middle and high school grades.

For example, if a student is caught graffiting the bathroom, they are often suspended. Whether it's in school or out of school suspension, they are missing important class discussions, the heart of learning.

Discipline through practical, natural methods can be much more effective than what they may consider a day "off." So, instead of kicking them out of their usual class routine and locking them in a detention room, or even worse, sending them home, why not try something else? Instead, have the student either come in early or stay late to clean their graffiti from the bathrooms with the janitor. They not only have consequences for their actions, but they also learn that they are going to be in charge of cleaning up or fixing it. This effect is the natural and reasonable result of the behavior that the student chose to participate in.

What's great about logical consequences is that they can be applied in so many areas. They are perfect for the classroom, with your own children, or for school wide policies. The consequences don't just punish; they teach, making this strategy a far better way to deal with unacceptable behavior. Making these situations into a proactive learning moment will stick with students far longer than punishment will.

Consequence vs. Punishment

According to professor and education expert John Shindler from California State University, there are definite differences between consequences and punishments.

Consequences:
- Intend to teach lessons
- Are logical and related
- Are proactive
- Promote responsibility
- Foster internal locus of control
- Work in the long run

Punishments:
- Intend to give discomfort
- Are unrelated and often personal
- Are reactive
- Can promote obedience, but sometimes also resentment
- Foster external locus of control
- Work in the short-term

3 Main Types of Logical Consequences

1. You Break It - You Fix It

Whether it was accidentally or intentionally, this deals with situations where something broke or a mess has been made. It assigns the student responsibility of righting the situation as best they can.

For example: A student running in the hallway knocks into another student, breaking their project for next period. Instead of sending the student to the office for punishment, have the student help fix the project. Then, have the student at fault explain to the teacher of that class that it was their fault for anything that may not have been fixable.

A student throws garbage instead of getting up to take it to the trash bin (or leaves scraps on the floor and walks out of the room when the period is over without cleaning up his/her area). Now, at the end of class, that student will have to stay for a minute and pick up any garbage on the floor in the room and get it all into the bin (or be on the recycling team for a week).

2. Loss of Privilege

This works great in the classroom to help dial in students' behavior. Adolescents are pretty much hardwired to challenge the rules at some point in time, and in doing so they have to face a consequence of losing a privilege.

For example: Students that didn't turn in their homework or complete the assignment will not get to participate in the fun activity or game that is planned. Instead, they have to spend that time to complete the work. Or, when a student fools around too much in class, he/she has to sit by the teacher for the rest of the class (or for an entire week).

3. A Positive Time Out

Sometimes students can't control themselves. They start to disrupt class with outbursts and other antics that hinder everyone's ability to learn in the classroom. That's when the student will need to "take a break" and recover self control. It is important that the students know this time-out is only to allow a chance to check their behavior before they spin out completely.

For example: A student won't stop talking out of turn during class, ignores instructions to be quiet, and keeps talking out of turn. Remove him/her from the immediate area to sit in a designated "time out spot" to calm down before it escalates. This chatty child is exactly the type of student who does not want to miss out on the community and discussion! The student will quickly learn to follow the guidelines for participation to avoid missing out again.

The key is to keep it streamlined, simple, and straightforward. Stay consistent, and use a calm voice to explain that now this is the consequence.

That's just how it works. Leave no room for argument or negotiation. Stay **calm** and **clear**.

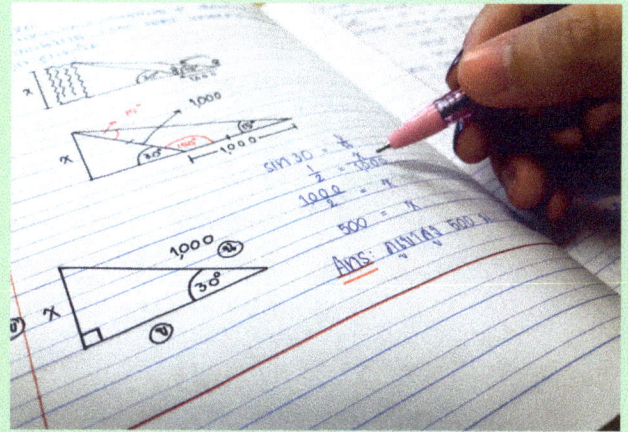

TIP: Whenever you prep a fun review game or activity, also copy a few simple worksheet versions that practice the same skill. This makes it so easy to keep the class under control during the fun activity or game. They'll know you always already have a more "boring" option ready for them, and a student who cannot handle the special lesson with self-control will be immediately handed the worksheet option and pulled from the class activity to go sit in the hall with a clipboard to do the quiet worksheet with the same type of practice. They will be motivated to stick to your expectations for behavior because they do not want the consequence of missing the fun.

Try phrases like:

"Clearly, you cannot handle this right now, so as a result, you'll need to grab that sheet from the corner of my desk and take it over to..."

"You will need to show me that you have the self-control to participate in an activity like this next time."

"Since you made the choice to ____, now you will have to _____."

"Now that you've caused ___(problem)___, you'll need to fix it by ___(natural consequence)___"

SPECIFIC EXAMPLES

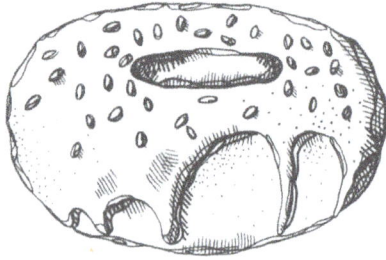

ingenuity invention & inspiration

WITH MRS. BRUZA

Recipe for a Middle School Teacher

a dash of sugar
1 lb. of sarcasm
36 quarts of spice
5 cups of planning
14 tbsp. of thick skin
543 gallons of coffee
97 pints of creativity
37 quarts of compassion
13,000 ounces of patience
14 tons of multitasking abilities

quotes and photos by Crystal Bruza
@MRSBRUZA

"Whenever someone finds out that I am a teacher, their first question is usually "What grade do you teach?" When I tell them that I am a middle school teacher, their reaction is generally something like, "Bless you Honey," or "I don't know how you do it," to which I always reply that I love it and wouldn't have it any other way. Teaching middle school is awesome! I relate most with the age group because they always tell it like it is, they have an outrageous sense of humor, they are eager to learn, and they have huge personalities. Every day is something different, so I am never bored. At this age, they also still have pretty big dreams and aren't afraid to share them. It's that fearlessness that inspires me on a daily basis. I learn as much from them as I hope they learn from me. Staying inspired year after year can be a challenge in any profession. Teaching is both mentally stimulating and challenging. This is my 14th year teaching middle school math, and one thing I strive for is to bring a sense of comfort and hominess to my classroom. With middle school students, they already have a lot going on. I would also be lying to myself if I thought every kid was going to walk into my room and enjoy math. I just always hope to make it as comfortable as possible, and I start every year telling my students that it is my goal to change how they feel about math. They don't have to love it, but my hope for them is that they at least like it (even if only a little). As a hobby, I enjoy crafting, so I try to incorporate things that I have made myself into my classroom. I find it makes it a more comfortable place for me as well, which is so important in my opinion. If you love what you do and you love where you do it, it's a win-win for both you and your students."

Wall files labeled by class period for both "turn in" papers and "pass back" papers make it easy to keep track of student work at both ends.

"Dressing up boring classroom windows is easy! Just cut some table runners in half and voila, you have window valances. I got these from Amazon! Super fun and easy."

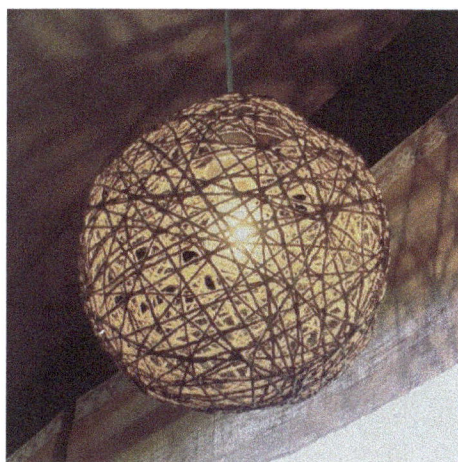

"One of my fave classroom decorations! I made this myself, and it was so much fun to do. You dip jute in wallpaper glue and wrap it around a beach ball leaving a spot open for the light to go in. Then you deflate the beach ball once it's all dry, pull the ball out, and voila: a really cool light!"

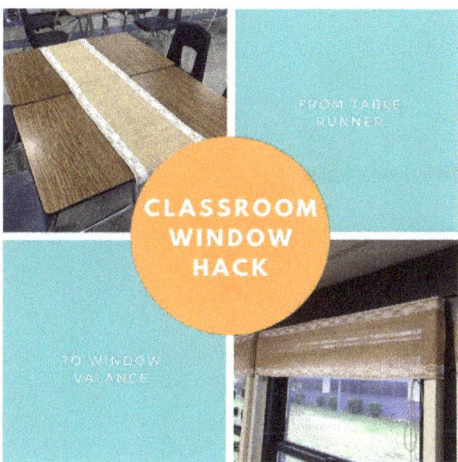

CLASSROOM WINDOW HACK

FROM TABLE RUNNER

TO WINDOW VALANCE

Crystal uses *Donors Choose* and also takes advantage of Amazon's "wishlist" option so parents and other contributors can easily donate just what she needs for her classroom. This funding helps her provide flexible seating and all the supplies and materials that she and her students need.

Creative use of materials keeps the classroom fresh. Crystal uses window clings on whiteboards. (They stick perfectly!) She has a variety of uses for washi tape to tag pencils, mark laptops, and build calendar grids on windows and boards. She takes full advantage of her bulletin boards to organize no-name papers and collect daily exit slips. As a crafty hack, instead of using paper or fabric, she sometimes covers the bulletin board with a beautiful shower curtain!

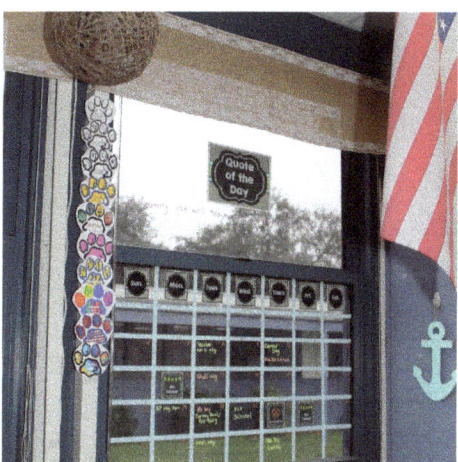

Blue sheeting covers the ceiling lights. These light diffuser covers soften the harsh fluorescent lighting and give the room a calmer feel.

"NAUTI profs"

Two Teachers Follow their Dream to Sail the World

DE SWAN

photos
and text
by
Karlijn
Ballemans

Life is boring without following your passions, is it not? Following your passions makes life worth it! Nowadays we spend most of our time in our jobs. That's why I chose a job I'm passionate about.

I started sailing when I was young, but not on a regular basis. During my studies some friends and I went sailing a few weekends a year, first in small open keel boats, and later in cabin boats. I always loved being out on the water, but I didn't live close enough to open water to sail on a regular basis.

During my last year of my teacher degree, I got the opportunity to become a teacher in the Masterskip program. Masterskip is an educational program in which students live aboard the tallship *Wylde Swan* for six weeks. They learn how to sail, continue their regular schoolwork and learn all about STEM topics related to life aboard. This project combines all my passions: sailing, traveling, teaching, and guiding students. Therefore, I paused my studies for a semester and in January 2015 I lived and worked for three months on the *Wylde Swan*.

We sailed from the Netherlands to the Caribbean. In the mornings, I helped the students with their regular schoolwork. In the afternoons, I taught them about geometry through coastal navigation, and in the evening I helped with sailing. After my trip I continued my studies, graduated and started working. My boss realised that Masterskip was important for me and approved that I could continue my travels on the *Wylde Swan* for 1 – 2 months every year. I worked 4 years for Masterskip and went on 5 trips including two ocean crossings (one from the Canary Islands to the Caribbean and one from Cuba to France), and some trips within the Caribbean.

On my third trip on the *Wylde Swan* I met Jordi, a biology teacher. He was also crazy about traveling, adventure and sailing. We fell in love. Our first date was on Dominica and our first kiss in St. Eustacia. Back in the Netherlands, things got serious. After awhile we started dreaming about our own sailing adventures. We subscribed ourselves for the Nautical college and studied all winter long to get our papers. Now, we have bought a boat and are sailing with it as much as we can while concretizing our plans to sail around the world together.

In one week I learnt the basics about sailing and I fell in love! I loved being out on the water. The fact that you can travel only on wind power intrigues me.

Instead of working as a teacher in a regular school, I'm working for an educational institute as an educational developer and mathematics teacher. My goal is to show people how cool STEM (Science, Technology, Engineering and Mathematics) can be. I develop educational material, and also give workshops, teacher trainings and advice related to STEM. This way I can express my creativity and work on my goal at the same time. As a teacher, I teach regular Math to high school students, but I also teach the Dutch language and didactics of mathematics to refugees who were teachers in their home countries and now want to become teachers in the Netherlands.

What got you interested in sailing, and how do you manage the practical aspects of this lifestyle?

When I was about 12 years old, I set foot on a sailing boat for the first time. It was on a sailing summer camp I went to with a friend. In one week I learnt the basics about sailing and I fell in love! I loved being out on the water. The fact that you can travel only on wind power intrigues me. Along with the peace and the calmness, it still does!

The key is to combine your passions and your job. I managed to get paid for teaching on a Tallship so I can afford to take unpaid leave from my regular job. Because I also sublet my apartment while I'm traveling, it doesn't cost me any money. While I'm in the Netherlands, I'm really enjoying my regular job. This gives me energy instead of draining my energy, which gives me enough energy to spend the weekends sailing.

Share a bit about your most fantastic travels. Are there any tips you can offer other teachers who have the deep desire to travel?

When I travel I always seek adventure and nature. Of course on top of my list are my travels on the *Wylde Swan* to the Caribbean, but I also made a fantastic journey through Norway with the Nomads bus. I travelled from Saint Petersburg all the way through Russia and Mongolia to Beijing. I travelled solo through Cuba, and travelled together with Jordi all the way from Czech Republic to Finland through Slovakia, Poland, Lithuania, Latvia and Estonia, and now we are planning to sail around the world.

Of course there are the regular holidays in which you can travel a lot. But if you want more, look around for opportunities to combine traveling with work. There are several educational sailing projects. It is also possible to work as a teacher abroad, for example in an international school like teachaway.com

Now you even have your own sailboat! Let us in on the behind-the-scenes secrets of sailing.

We have an Halcyon 27, a small cabin boat of 27 feet. It's a classic English yacht from 1978. We bought it for just 2000 euro and fixed it up. It's a polyester boat with teak details. It has everything we need: autopilot, electric card system, living area (with headroom), a kitchen, a toilet, and a double bed in the front. It has

teaching the math behind coastal navigation

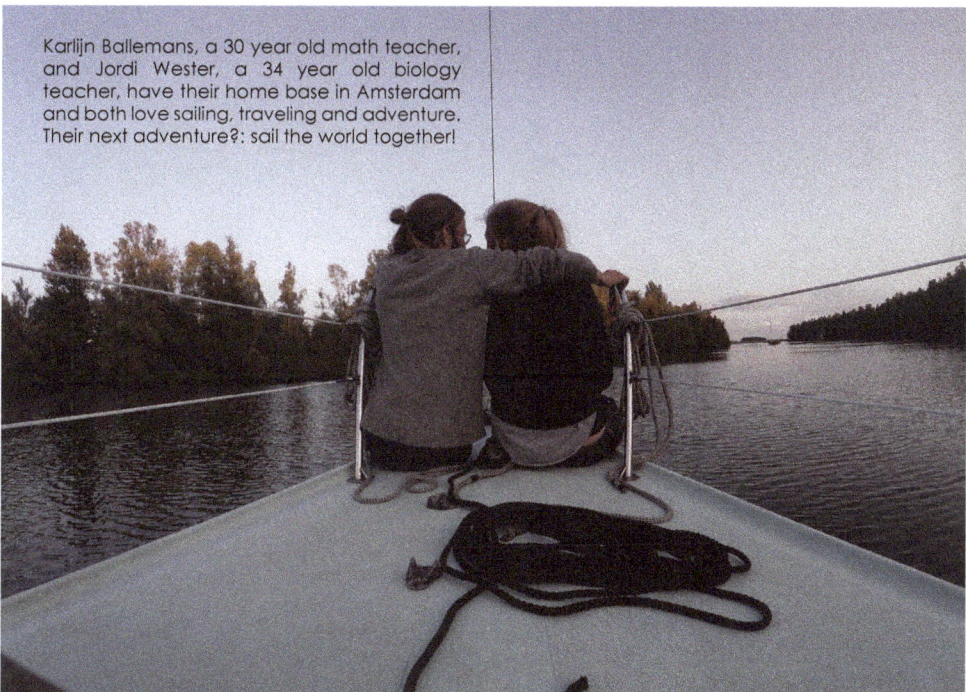
Karlijn Ballemans, a 30 year old math teacher, and Jordi Wester, a 34 year old biology teacher, have their home base in Amsterdam and both love sailing, traveling and adventure. Their next adventure?: sail the world together!

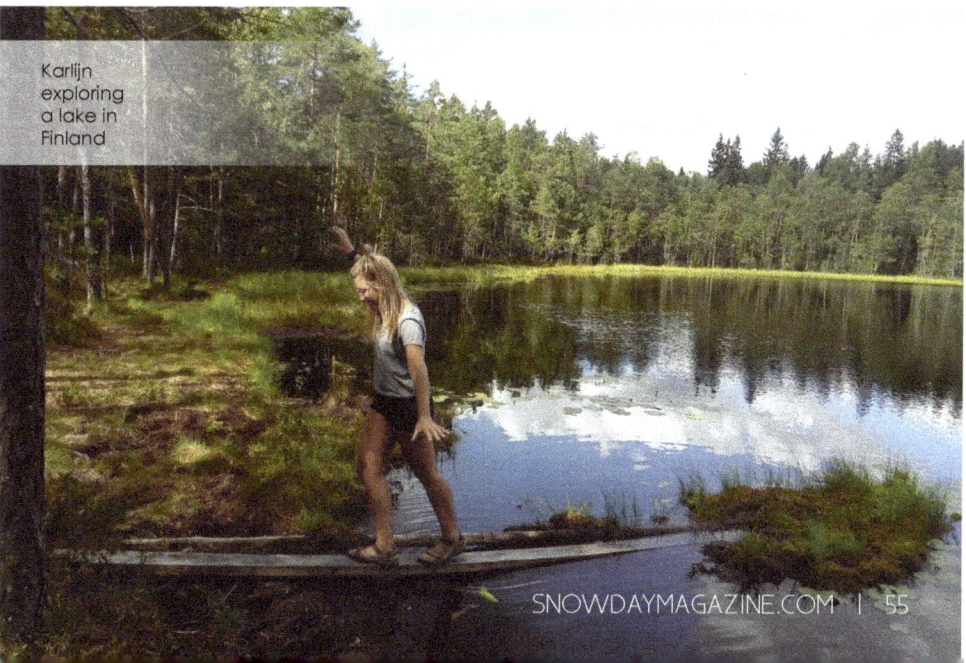
Karlijn exploring a lake in Finland

> *Students learn so much more when they get the chance to go out there, explore, learn by doing, and challenge themselves by doing research and designing solutions for problems within subjects that matter to them.*

the lovely name 'Dare II Dream' in Disney letters (no kidding). We're still thinking of a new name. Tips are welcome! (mail to nautiprofs@gmail.com)

People have a quite romantic image about sailing. And of course, it can be very romantic to be out at sea, dolphins around your bow, the most beautiful sunsets, the clearest sky full of stars, etcetera. But it isn't always so romantic. While living on a sailboat, your home is always moving, so you can't put anything on the table or it will fall off. Stuff is breaking all the time, and maintenance of the boat is like a full time job. In heavy weather it is not possible to cook. Even going to the bathroom can be a big challenge. You roll out of your bed while sailing. You have to be alert all the time. You get the picture.

When on board, I always wake up before Jordi. I start to fry eggs on our little stove and make coffee with the percolator. While the coffee is on the stove, I check the weather. Is there enough wind today? From which direction does the wind come? What route are we going to take today? The smell of fresh coffee and fried eggs lures my boyfriend out of his bed, and we start having breakfast together outside in the sun. After breakfast, we jump into the water for a shower, then we hoist the sails!

Tell us all about the next exciting adventure!

One of the most important challenges for education nowadays is to adjust to the modern times. Still a lot of schools offer outdated education that's not working anymore for the modern kids. Students learn so much more when they get the chance to go out there, explore, learn by doing, and challenge themselves by doing research and designing solutions for problems within subjects that matter to them. In the Netherlands, most people involved in education seem to realize this. But making the step to do something about it is something totally different. The politicians

and most schoolboards are afraid to make the wrong changes and are therefore quite conservative. The world is changing so fast. However, the educational system does not seem to take advantage of this out of fear.

We have BIG plans! By the end of this school year, both Jordi and I are quitting our jobs. We are going to sail the world indefinitely. On the way we will visit schools all over the world to get inspired and learn by their way of education. We are starting a foundation. Our passion is to spread explorative and practical education around the world by making an educational journey with our sailing boat.

While visiting schools and refugee camps around the world, we will share our stories, enthusiasm, and experiences to inspire others for explorative, practical education. We will offer educational material, teacher trainings and workshops/lessons. This includes letting students in international schools explore the math behind sailing, helping them to discover the world of micro-organisms in the ocean, and even letting children in refugee camps experience how to design and program their own robots.

Follow our journey via Instagram or Facebook @nautiprofs or contact us via email (nautiprofs@gmail.com).

recommended resources

Educational Sailing Projects:
masterskip.com
classafloat.com
schoolatsea.com

Nomad Bus
letsbenomads.com

Educational Institute
wismon.nl

teachers with a dream

Have you always dreamt about working abroad, traveling for a while, starting your own business? Whatever it is, go for it!

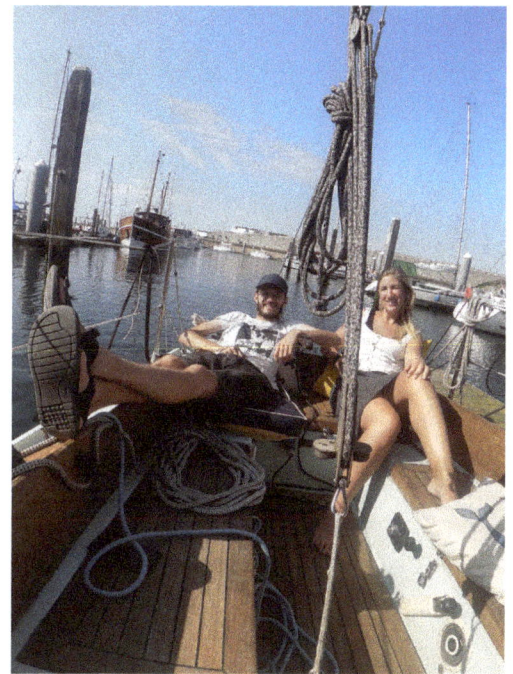

gratitude

I'm most grateful that I have the luxury to do what I'm passionate about, that I can follow my dreams, and that I found somebody who is crazy enough to follow them with me.

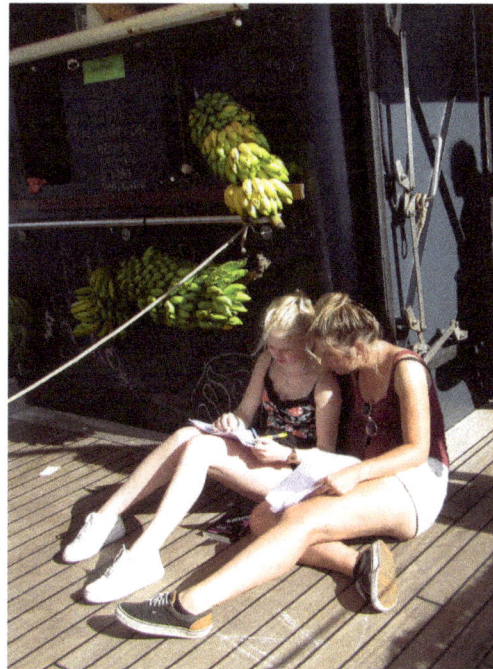

my mentor

was my math teacher from the fifth grade. In the beginning I didn't like him at all. I just wanted to chat with my friends; why should I be interested in math? He challenged me to put effort into math and showed me that math can be interesting and fun. He is one of the reasons I studied math after high school.

sailing

these pages from left to right:

>> Karlijn on a hike in Norway

>> Karlijn sailing on the North Sea

>> Jordi and Karlijn in their own sailboat

>> Karlijn helping a student with her math on the Wylde Swan

>> Jordi collecting clams from the bottom of the ocean

>> sailing on a little sailboat in Bermuda

@nautiprofs

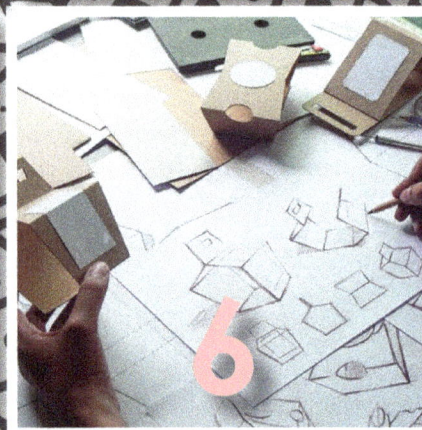

DISCOVER

Everything on Instagram you had no idea you needed to know about!

1 >> @misscraftymathteacher

Kathleen is passionate about combining creativity and student engagement. Her simple, yet genius teacher hacks and fun activities are developed for her own high school math classroom in Houston, but many of her unique strategies can be applied over a wide range of grade levels.

2 >> @chemix.app

The free software at chemix.org allows teachers or students to draw up lab diagrams. Simply choose items like beakers, bunsen burners, tongs, funnels, pipettes, thermometers, etc. and easily drop the elements into a diagram. Even options like bubbles, ice cubes, and timers are available to demonstrate a customized step-by-step set of graphic directions.

3 >> @tools_n_tiaras

The Tools & Tiaras organization inspires and mentors girls who are interested in the trades. They are striving to "forge" strong girls by allowing them to gain hands-on experience in mechanical, industrial, and technical trades. They offer automotive workshops, let girls learn to use real power tools, run construction skills summer camps, and give practice in plumbing, building, masonry, welding, and more.

4 >> @novel_effect

Novel Effect is a free app that adds character voices, music, and sound effects to enhance a story being read aloud. Stories offered in Spanish are being added now as well. Little ones will love the additions while you read them the story, and you'll be amazed at how well it keeps up with your voice.

5 >> @toocoolformiddleschool

Megan teaches middle school, but she also guides teachers who are navigating current issues inside and outside the world of education. She is a wonderful resource for finding ethical fashion options, battling racism, and working towards social justice. Our favorite places to follow along with her are on Instagram and YouTube.

6 >> @howlifeunfolds

This Instagram account, managed by "Paper & Packaging: How life unfolds" is surprisingly inspirational. Gather ideas for papercrafting, explore package design, and get your creative wheels turning. One of their instructional downloads this past school year was a fun back-to-school countdown calendar made with a variety of crafty supplies.

HOT LEMON WATER

first thing in the morning is said to wake up your digestive system, brighten your mood, and aid your immune system and metabolism.

STANDING DESKS

keep our bodies less sedentary. Set some up for students, and get yourself an adjustable desktop stand so you can alternate between sitting and standing.

WEAVING

is a soothing hobby where the hands can work while the brain rests. If a loom is not yet in your life, consider a simple starter kit for weekend crafting.

BATTLE "TECH EYES"

with AREDS 2 vitamins. Help prevent macular degeneration from viewing screens all day with a blend that includes lutein and zeaxanthin.

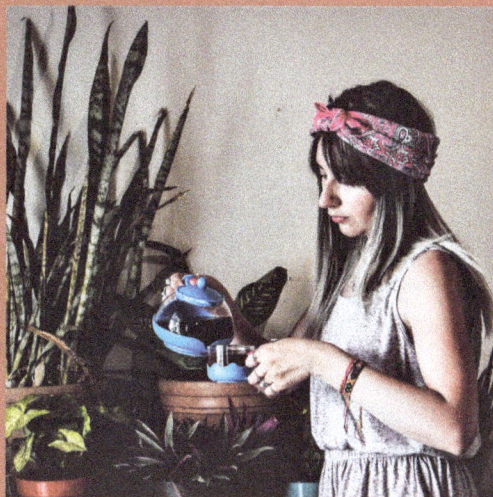

ADAPTOGENIC COFFEE

can help regulate stress systems in the body. Always check with your doctor before trying herbal blends or changing up your supplement routines.

CAFE VIBES

at school help some older students relax and gain independence. Classrooms or allotted times that mimic a workplace help them practice productivity.

TRIBAL PATTERNS

are trending. Give your classroom, teacher outfits, and home decor a global appeal with kilim textiles, kantha cloth, indigo, or southwestern patterns.

AVOCADO TREES

can be grown in your own home. If you can't get enough guacamole and avocado toast, try planting one to harvest any time you wish!

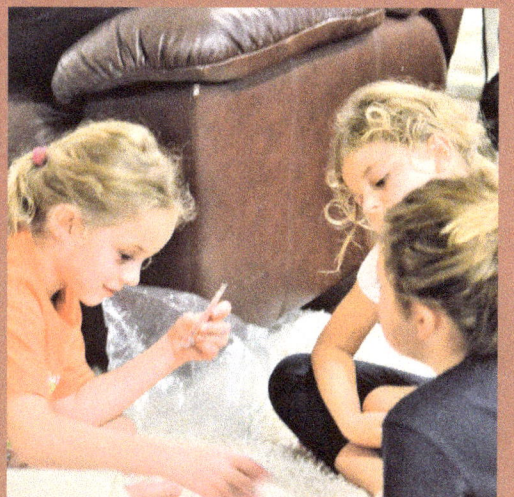

COOPERATIVE GAMES

allow students to work as a team but still have the benefits of game play. They get a competitive challenge, but work toward/against it collaboratively.

natural HOMES

Splurge on a beautiful natural tile, but only a small amount. This real Carrara Bianca marble mosaic was about $10 per square foot. It would be cost prohibitive for most people to tile an entire bathroom with, but all that was needed to tile this stair riser was a sheet and a half. This quick and easy project was budget friendly and finished in just a few minutes, then grouted the next day.

Total cost of material: about $35 including mastic and grout

Tips: Do not spend money to rent a tile saw for this size of mosaic tile. Tile nippers work perfectly and are easy to use to trim the few tiles that need cutting on each end. Everything you need is easy to find at the hardware store. Use the smallest trowel and grout float available, and be sure to choose unsanded grout so the marble will not scratch in the process.

marble

DIY
baby steps on a budget

Natural products are gorgeous, but can be expensive. These tiny projects make a big impact by helping just a small amount of real material go a long way.

Don't underestimate nature's most valuable influence on your home. Natural light is free, so take advantage and maximize its impact. It can be well worth the cost to replace your front door with one that has small windows, or to get blinds that will replace heavy, old drapes, and let light in. Play tricks with the light to spice up your space. You can add a sparkle to any room by adding a mirrored ball placed a few feet away from a window, or add a glow by installing a simple sheer curtain in just the right spot.

light

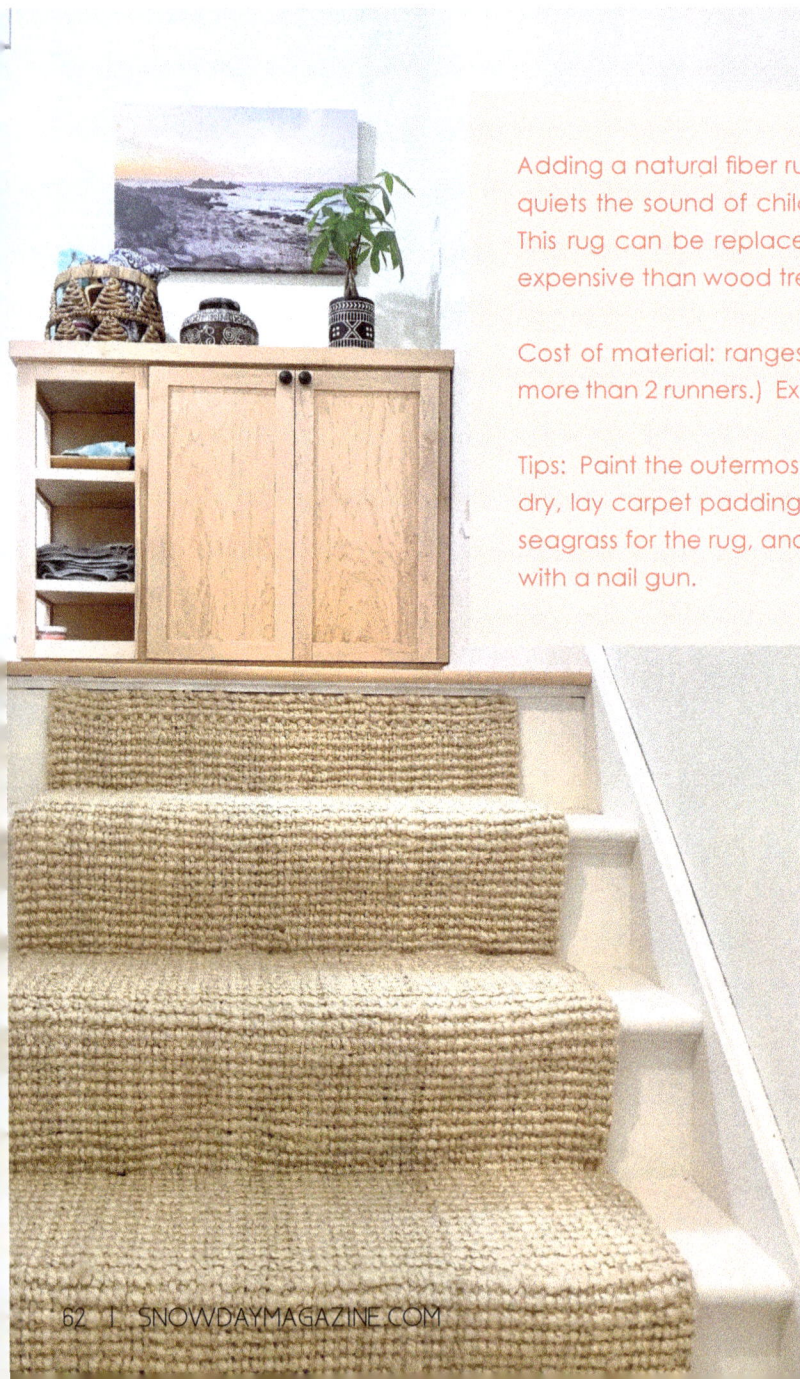

Adding a natural fiber runner on a staircase gives it texture and cushioning. It also quiets the sound of children scampering up and down creaky old wooden stairs. This rug can be replaced more easily than full carpeting, and is significantly less expensive than wood treads that would match the hardwood flooring.

Cost of material: ranges from $30 - $65 per runner (A full staircase requires a little more than 2 runners.) Extra rug segments can be used in another area of the house.

Tips: Paint the outermost 8 inches of each stair with a durable floor paint. When it's dry, lay carpet padding on each tread before attaching the rug. Try jute, sisal, or seagrass for the rug, and look for 18 gauge 1/4 inch crown 1 1/4 inch staples to use with a nail gun.

fiber

Can't afford a granite countertop or fancy marble floor? Focus on the accents and accessories. These small doses of natural material offer a touch of glamour. Display a granite mortar and pestle, mango wood candle holders, seagrass baskets, a marble lazy susan, plently of plants, and cane or wicker accents.

tiny touches

A cutom fit modern wall panel does double duty by warming up the tv area and hiding the cords, which are tucked neatly behind the central wooden slat. The inexpensive plywood backer board was cut into two pieces to leave a tall channel down the middle. The cords drop down through the niche and are hidden, but still accessible by removing one slat. The board behind the slats was painted a dark charcoal color to enhance the shadow effect, and the strips nailed to it are natural maple.

Total cost of material: about $40

Tip: Add a small piece of trim molding at the bottom, where the panel meets the floor or a cabinet. This will finish the look and disguise any imperfect cuts.

wood

getting started with

gamification

Gamifying is not simply playing games in your classroom. Gamification is incentivizing desired behavior with points, levels, and rewards.

by Leah Cleary

>> high school teacher
>> tech expert
>> blended learning blogger

leahcleary.com

how it works

Gamifying is a fun classroom management strategy. It's the way many apps, programs, and even businesses are starting to work. But gamifying is not simply playing games in your classroom. Gamification is incentivizing desired behavior with points, levels, and rewards.

Let's say you teach a math class, and you want your students to bring their notebooks and pencils (or 1:1 devices) every day. Give them a point for doing that. These points don't go into the gradebook, though. They're part of the larger game around which you have structured your classroom. After a certain number of points, students will move up a level, or "level-up."

Each level holds with it a desired privilege. That privilege can be a simple reward or "skill" that the student now possesses. Each level is associated with a badge.

This is how video games work. It's how various apps that incentivize weight loss and healthy lifestyles work. (Think about the badges you earn on your Fitbit). This is the way many offices work, as well, so it's no wonder that classrooms are headed in the same direction.

why gamify?

I've been in the classroom for almost 20 years, and I believe I have a pretty good grasp on the management side. I'm good at developing a rapport with my students and at making my lessons engaging (I hope). What's more, I'm not a very organized person, nor am I a gamer.

So why does gamification make sense for me? Gamification is the direction the world is heading for a very simple reason -- because it works. It works because it combines the right amount of collaboration with competition. It recognizes progress over grades, and effort over results. It makes it okay to try and fail because badges, rewards, and recognition come from the effort -- the process. We don't always have to be perfect in a gamified classroom.

For example, I hate exercising, but I know I should do it because it's good for me. That knowledge had not been enough to get me to do it in the past, but when I bought a Fitbit, I could see tangible results for the progress I had made. I would earn badges for taking extra steps. Seeing the steps my friends had taken on a given day encouraged me to take more. I'm cheering for them, but I'm also competing with them. I may not see immediate physical results from taking 10,000 steps in a day, but I will see fireworks on my Fitbit.

Those simple fireworks work! They give me an immediate sense of accomplishment. I want to keep on progressing because that makes me feel good. Accomplishing goals, solving problems, working with others, and being recognized releases the dopamine in my brain that encourages me to keep going, even when I don't necessarily feel like it.

Transferring this idea to your classroom can make your students feel the same way. It might seem overwhelming at first, but it's worth it in the long run.

avatars

On the first day of school, have each student design their avatar and use it to describe themselves briefly to the class. This will serve as a "getting to know you" activity as well as serve a purpose in your game.

The no-tech option is to use an avatar sheet. Students can either draw their avatars or cut out images from magazines to put one together. Then they can hang them on the wall. The tech option is to have students design one using an app such as photos-share.com which is free in the Chrome Web Store and incredibly easy to use. They can save the avatar as an image and insert it into a Google Slide™ that you've shared with the class as "can edit" so that students can add their own slide, insert their avatar, and use it to briefly describe themselves. You can project it for the class and keep it in the "About" section of Google Classroom™ or whatever digital platform you use. Before doing that, though, make a copy and simply share it so that students can no longer edit.

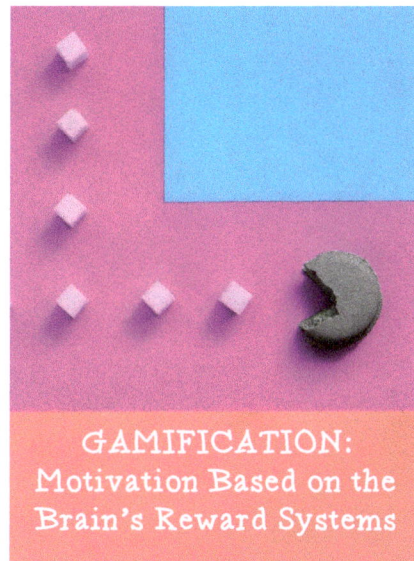

GAMIFICATION:
Motivation Based on the
Brain's Reward Systems

xp and leveling up

The first thing you'll need to do in order to gamify your classroom is to consider behaviors you would like to reinforce in your students. I would recommend concrete behaviors. Things like kindness and generosity are great, but they're far too difficult to quantify. They are also difficult to notice on every occasion.

It's vital that your students buy into this, and if they feel like you've been unfair, they'll give up. For example, a student may see you reward another for something he believes he did and you ignored. That's not good because he will no longer see any purpose in continuing to play.

Next, decide how many points each of these will be worth. I use game-language, so I call the points "experience" (XP).

For my own classroom, I decided on 10 levels. The first is very easy to achieve in order to award students right off the bat and encourage

"buy in." Level 10 is very difficult to achieve, and nobody may reach it at all. That's okay. Reaching level 10 should be a big deal. In order to encourage collaboration as well as competition, it's a good idea to reward an entire class or a group when everyone in that class or group reaches, say, level 5.

In order to encourage interest, it's also a good idea to throw random challenges in. For example, if you want your students to check Google Classroom or Blackboard, or whatever LMS you use, you could post something like, "Comment on this post for 3 XP before such and such a time." Students should never get too comfortable. Randomness keeps things interesting.

Think of one day a week to have a "Leveling-Up Ceremony." It could be Monday, Friday, or any day in between. I think Monday is the best because you have the weekend to enter XP into your spreadsheet and award badges. The ceremony can be short. It can involve checking badges digitally or having the students place badges on their avatar sheets if you're not using tech. Announce the "skill" each student now has. They can use their skill immediately or save it for a later date. (See "Skills" chart on next page).

I use *Flippity* for leveling up. *Flippity* is a Google Sheets Add-On. I have cheat sheets and tutorials at leahcleary.com that explain how to use *Flippity*. When students use their skill for each level, I place an asterisk next to it on the *Flippity* Badge spreadsheet so that a star appears on their badge, and we know they've used their skill's reward.

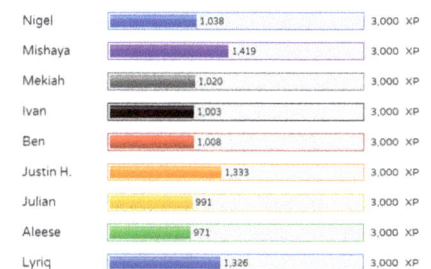

Nigel	1,038	3,000 XP
Mishaya	1,419	3,000 XP
Mekiah	1,020	3,000 XP
Ivan	1,003	3,000 XP
Ben	1,008	3,000 XP
Justin H.	1,333	3,000 XP
Julian	991	3,000 XP
Aleese	971	3,000 XP
Lyriq	1,326	3,000 XP

The leaderboard is created very simply from a Google sheet using the free "Flippity" Add-On. For details, visit leahcleary.com

the quest

It's fun to center your gamified classroom around a quest that only the students can achieve. (There's

skills

Each level comes with a specific skill. Each skill comes with a reward that the students may use once. Here are the skills and rewards I came up with:

1. Strength
Choose a piece of candy or a selection from the school supply bin (see Game Card Section).

2. Stealth
Pick a Friday to sit where you want.

3. Mobility
Earn one extra restroom pass.

4. Healing
Get +50 XP for yourself or to divide among your group.

5. Invisibility
Enjoy 10 minutes of screen time on a Friday.

6. Wisdom
Select one assignment to skip.

7. Magic
Add 10 points to the assignment of your choice.

8. Invincibility
Drop your lowest grade.

9. Courage
Spin the wheel for extra points.

10. All-Powerful
Get one reward from each skill level.

Notice that as students move up levels, their reward starts to impact their grade. They've done a lot of extra work to achieve the higher levels, so that seems fair to me.

Gamification works because it combines the right amount of collaboration with competition. It recognizes progress over grades, effort over results. It makes it okay to try and fail because badges, rewards, and recognition come from the effort--the process.

psychology behind the "only you" statements that video games use to hook players all the time.) Since my class is world history, and we begin with the birth of civilization, the quest is about stopping the fall of civilization. Each unit challenge centers around a real-world problem that could lead to civilization's collapse, including problems such as fake news, global warming, terrorism, and feeding the population. Groups must consider solutions to these problems. One group in each class wins the challenge and the XP that goes along with it.

game cards

Game cards add an element of randomness. During class, I may offer a group challenge or offer one as a prize for winning a game, or even, as a weekly reward, spin the wheel and reward one to the student on whose name it lands.

I have XP Cards, for which students can be rewarded up to 10 additional XPs, and Loot Cards. The Loot Cards say things like, "bin 1, "bin 3," "candy," or "free answer."

I keep four bins in my closet at school. One bin contains candy, one school supplies like pencils, lead, and highlighters, one fun things like adult coloring and sudoku books, and the last contains technology prizes like earbuds, chargers, and screen wipes. I've accumulated these things from Dollar Stores, clearance shelves, and donations, and they

Available Badges

Select a name to view badges earned.

Demetrice	Daniella	Kelly	Olivia
Nigel	Mishaya	Mekiah	Ivan
Ben	Justin H.	Julian	Aleese
Lyriq	Ava	Justin L.	Labron
Cameron	Jabari	Michelle	Savannah
Mariyah	T.J.	Faiz	Ce Ce
Jelani	Kylee	Glenn	Kieran

This badge-tracker is created very simply from a Google Sheet using the free Flippity Add-On. For more information, visit leahcleary.com.

For the Weekly Wheel, add students' names who met certain requirements the previous week and spin for a winner.

These wheels are created very simply from a Google Sheet using the free Flippity Add-On. For more information, visit leahcleary.com.

One free prize that they love is the chance to spin for extra XP.

aren't awarded often. Giving away too much cheapens the awards (plus it can get expensive). But the very best rewards are free. The Loot Cards also offer a free answer on a test or a quiz.

staying organized

This is my biggest weakness; I'll admit it. But most of my XP is centered around things I must do anyway, like tardies and attendance.

What works for me is to print out a seating chart for each class each week. I mark down the points right on it as students earn them. Then on Friday afternoon, I take half an hour to enter the points into the online spreadsheet. The colors of the totals let me know if students have leveled up. (I set the spreadsheet to auto add and change colors when certain totals are reached.)

I use Google Sheets to keep track of the data. I have sheets that I use to keep up with weekly XP, another sheet that communicates that information to a Leaderboard, and another that communicates the information to a badge tracker. I link the sheets together so that I only have to enter XP into one of the sheets and it automatically communicates with the others. I have a tutorial and cheat sheets for doing this at leahcleary.com.

On Monday mornings, I project the flippity.net link and recognize each student who has gained a level. Usually, the students have already seen it because I keep a link to it in the "About" section of Google Classroom™. They can't wait to check it.

You can also embed leaderboards and badge trackers on a Google Site or your school's Learning Management System. If I wasn't using technology, I would hang student avatar sheets on the wall, and have each student who leveled up stick the new badge beneath their avatar.

and remember ...

We need to model for our students that true learning doesn't just happen. It takes hard work, it takes starts and stops, and it takes failure.

Success doesn't come from playing it safe, but standardized tests and grades in school reinforce in our students that it does.

It's time to turn that notion on its head.

Since I don't tie gamification in my classroom to grades, it helps students do just that: Take risks. Fail. Try again. Be creative. True, rewards can impact grades in the higher levels, but it goes beyond that.

Students earn experience points (XP) by coming to class prepared, being on time, putting their phones away, completing creative extension assignments, problem-solving, coming in for extra help, retaking tests and quizzes, and so on. Gamification naturally fosters a growth mindset, so don't be afraid to try this method. It won't be perfect at first, but that's how we learn.

Get support for getting started at leahcleary.com

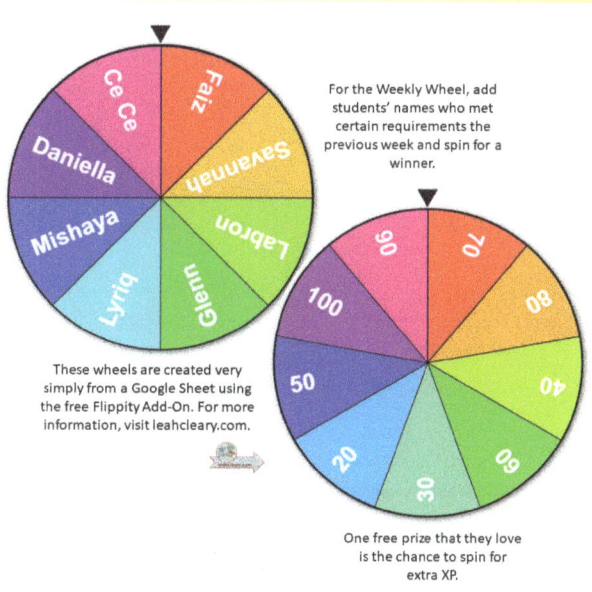

natural nuances

Ms. Gossett Brings a Bohemian Twist to Third Grade

Natural fibers, plants, and layers upon layers of neutral textiles lend a cozy appeal to what used to be a standard issue classroom in South Carolina.

This is my V.I.P chair for my class. Students acheive this when they have gone above and beyond. They love their flexible seating. They never let me forget to change the rotation. It means so much more to them to be sitting around the room rather than sitting at their desks.

This is one of my favorite spots because of how comfy it is. This is one of our flexible seating options. Each group gets a different seat assignment every week where they sit during workshops. I got my couch from Facebook Market, and got quite a few things from Five Below.

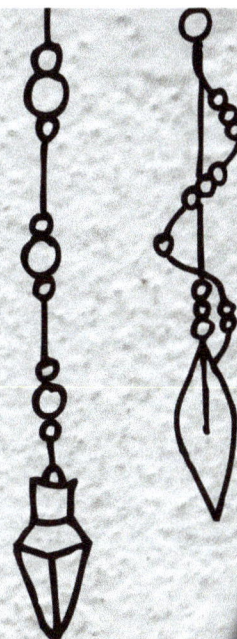

words & photography by M. Gossett @3rdgradesthecharm_

servant hearts

I am a 3rd grade teacher (all subjects). I am a first year teacher in Spartanburg, SC. I just graduated last May from Anderson University, the school I always dreamed of going to. I met my fiancee at Anderson and I'm getting married in March. I am very extra when it comes to everything, from wearing the biggest earrings to having my classroom a certain way.

I think that I have created a classroom that is conducive to learning. It's so different having your own classroom! I have dreamed forever of having my own and what it would look like, so when I got hired, I already had an idea that I wanted my classroom to look more like a home than a classroom.

I got a lot of things from Amazon, but also had a lot of decorations from the house I lived in during college. I try my best to make a warm, inviting environment for students to feel at home in. My students are so respectful and loving, and have such servant hearts. They have been the biggest blessing in my first year of teaching.

This is the corner of the room where I hide my junk with cute cube organizers and a table skirt.

natural fiber macrame wall hangings

succulents in unique plant hangers

Himalayan salt lamp with a warm glow

living plants spread out in beautiful pots

calming neutral colors from nature

MISTAKES HELP US GROW

healing, peace, and grace

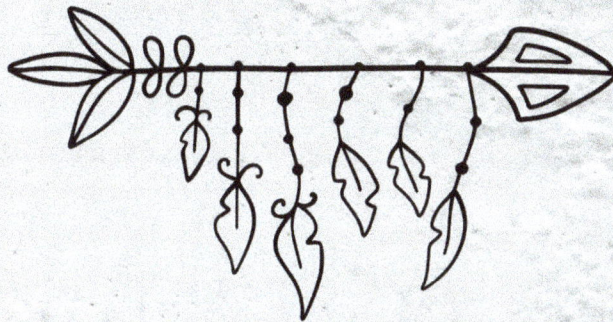

It is very important that I take the time to ask for healing and peace through the school year and have the right mindset. I do this by trying to always have God's guidance in everything I do. Another way I make sure to nurture my whole self is by not putting myself as the victim. For example: "we don't get paid enough," "I shouldn't have to deal with this as a first year," "we don't have enough say in school decisions."

These are all examples that normal teachers think everywhere, but if I start to fill myself with those thoughts that I am just not appreciated, it can cause self inflicted stress and anxiety that I don't have to have. I am so undeserving of the grace that I have been given in my life. Keeping those thoughts away keeps me wanting to wake up and go to my job.

I love to read any kind of Christian books that have to do with becoming more of a woman of God. My relationship with the Lord has such an impact in everything I do: the way I treat my kids, the way I treat my family, and the way I think of myself. Other than that, as self care, I get on kicks of crafting when I find something I think I can make myself.

My room stays spotless because at the beginning of the year I made it an expectation that it would begin and end clean. My kids are so respectful of that and LOVE cleaning up for me and helping me. They do little things like rinse out my coffee cup and put it in my lunch box without me noticing. They beg to carry my water bottle that I take everywhere.

They know I don't like a cluttered desk. They will stack my papers and put everything back in its place. They see this as a privilege, and it really helps. I do realize that I won't always have the same dynamic in the years to come, and that not all kids like to clean (lol).

This is the first time something has really been mine. I got a lot of help along the way. It's so encouraging to know that I set the tone for how my students treat each other.

keeping it clutter-free

I spend most of my time behind my kidney table or sitting on my fuzzy chair. I saw the wonderful idea to have a skirt for my kidney table, and that has helped so much with it not feeling cluttered. (I hide a lot of junk under my table that no one can see.) I have snacks that I keep in drawers so I don't go hungry or end up getting something from the vending machine.

At one of our first meetings with first year teachers, someone said "Fake it till you make it." That really stuck with me because as teachers, we have a never ending to-do list. I have so much to learn and sometimes I can't go through the list of all of the things I haven't done.

To find balance between work and life, the simplest way is not bringing work home with me. I stay at school until I'm finished, instead of not being present around my family. This is easier said than done, but it has been so helpful in my first year. My school has a wonderful impact on me. I have a great team that I work with. They are always there to encourage me and give me the best resources and guidance. If I didn't have great teachers to work with, I imagine my first year would feel pretty lonely.

I am most grateful for my fiancee and family. They have helped me transition into this year of changes.

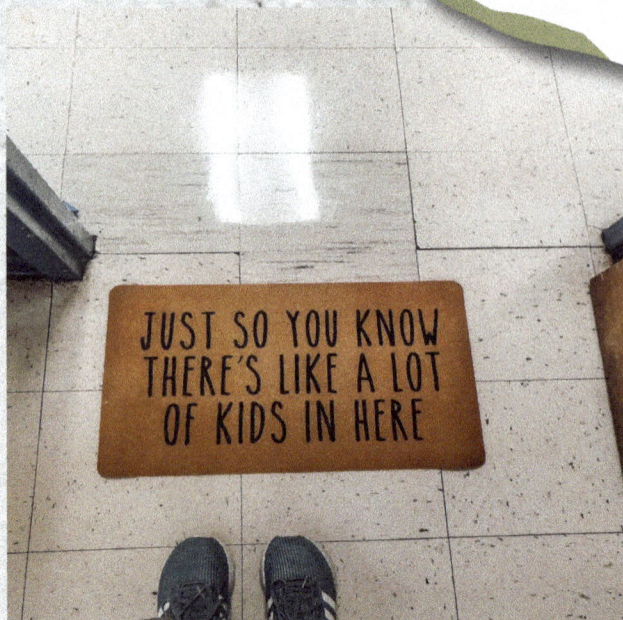

I moved out the generic teacher desk and brought this in from my parents' basement. I wanted the extra space, so this small desk was the perfect fit.

It is very important that I take the time to ask for healing and peace through the school year and have the right mindset.

Ms. Gosset's Five Sanity-Saving Tips for Teachers

we have the best job in the world

1 >> If you end up being gassy one day, always blame it on the students, because teachers NEVER pass gas.

2 >> You don't have to grade everything. Don't be afraid to toss it!

3 >> Enjoy the small moments.

4 >> Never be afraid to ask for help. No one has it all together.

5 >> Take at least one personal day each semester; you deserve a day of rest.

terra cotta

Italian artist Marco Zagaria engineered and designed a dome shaped terra cotta heater that takes only five minutes to heat up and requires the power of only four tealight candles to heat an entire room.

Students in Hong Kong built a terra cotta tower to demonstrate the possibilities of 3d printing in architecture.

A hospital in San Antonio, Texas displays a facade of glass protected by shade strips made from terra cotta that represent the way skin grafts can similarly protect a human burn victim from the sun.

Clearly, terra cotta is an actively used material in a variety of design and engineering applications today. Its ancient history, versatility, and attractive character are still drawing the eye.

"BAKED EARTH"

EARTHY WARM TONES

The rough and rustic appeal of terra cotta has made the material popular for generations. Terra cotta, or "baked earth" in Italian, has a history of more than 4,000 years. Artisans across the globe have been producing a variety of creations using this versatile earthen medium since before 2000 BC.

Clay is fired at high temperatures, causing a vitrification process that helps it fuse together, making this natural material durable and weatherproof.

The possibilities of terra cotta as a material range from European roofs to a Chinese army of soldier statues. Experiment with plant pots, dishes, trays, and tiles in your own home, but be aware that when we consider terra cotta as simply a color, it has even more promise.

Warm up your trendy grey or white home with this unique color that can even act as another neutral. The muted orange hues of terra cotta offer a textured conterbalance to your home.

Accent Wall

Terra cotta colored paint offers a perfect backdrop for a variety of colors and creates a cohesive look in a room. It is bold enough to make your home stand out, yet neutral enough to play smoothly with your furnishings.

Color Combos

There's a reason that terra cotta is such a hot choice for plant pots. It looks great with many shades of green. Try a silvery sage green, a mint green, or even a bright tone if you enjoy saturated color. Test swatches with more pink tones as well as browner ones to see what coordinates best with your decor.

Greenery

Enhance the appeal of terra cotta surfaces or coloring with plenty of foliage. Plants are always the perfect accent to any room, but work particularly well with these tones. The greenery will effortlessly soften the hard, coarse material and complement the organic feel.

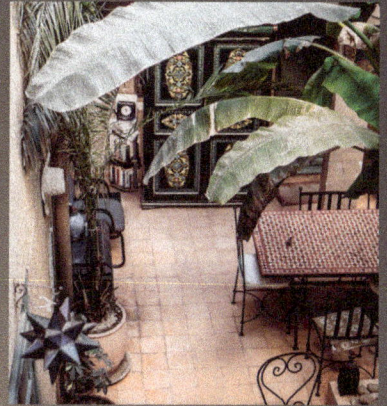

Global Vibes

Terra cotta stands out beautifully against white, but you can also layer vivid colors against it. If you can incorporate plenty of bold jewel tones in the space, this chameleon-like color will lend a global influence to a space, evoking themes similar to a Morrocan riad or Spanish courtyard.

Small Doses

You may not be ready to embrace a full wall of paint yet, but try a textile or two. Throw blankets, pillows, rugs, and wall hangings are a great way to get a softer sampling of the warmth of burnt earth.

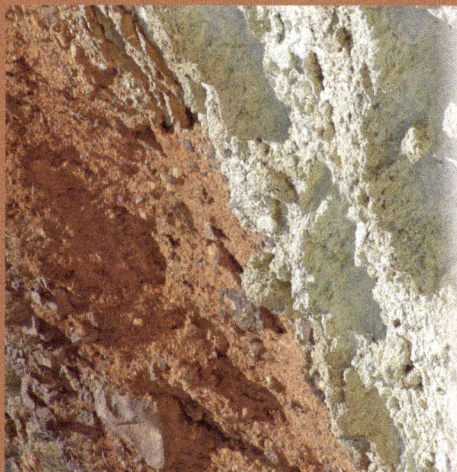

A Range of Options

Are you a fan of millenial pink? Or do you prefer orange or brown tones? There is a range of terra cotta hues. All are colors that occur naturally in the clay and give off an earthy allure.

inspiration

LAUREN'S EARTHY BLEND
@LAURENANDLOFT

PHOTOS AND TEXT
BY LAUREN MCGEE

SEE MORE OF LAUREN'S HOME IDEAS ON INSTAGRAM: @LAURENANDLOFT

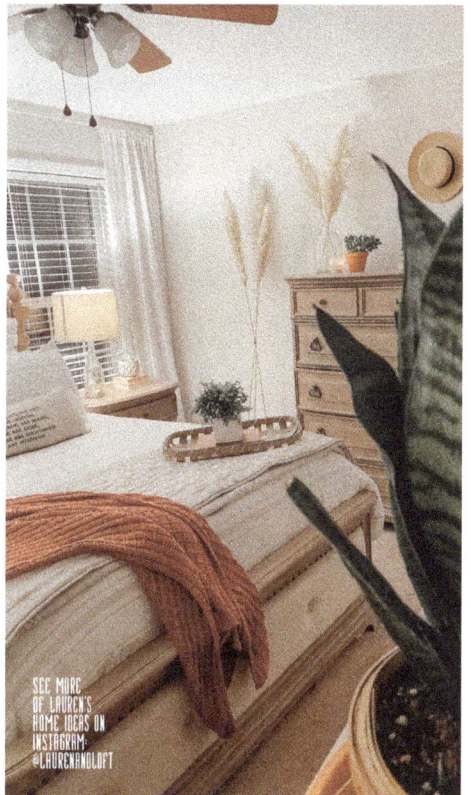

Terra Cotta Tones

I used to believe everything had to be monochromatic. Everything in my house was a shade of gray. It wasn't until this past year that I started getting into house plants, and the terracotta pots looked great with the greenery. That was what really inspired me to start adding some bolder colors and prints into my home.

I think terra-cotta serves as a great neutral. It's definitely on the bold side of the spectrum as far as neutrals go, but it is so versatile. It pairs well with green, it pairs great with burgundy, and I even love it with a good mustard yellow. There is a way to incorporate it into any season.

One day I was at Lowe's shopping for plants and came across the section with all sorts of terra-cotta pots and saucers. The saucers were cheap and I knew instantly that I could paint them and they would look great hanging up on my walls. I just used a white paint pen and sketched simple geometric designs on to them. For hanging, I used the adhesive command strips. It was one of the simplest DIY's I've ever done.

Creativity Expressed through Home Styling

I work full time as an ICU nurse. I received my nursing degree while on an art scholarship (I've always been an artist). I am currently teaching myself to paint hyper-realistic paintings, which means that they should resemble something close to a photograph and not an actual painting.

I'd say my style is a mix of boho/traditional/modern. I don't really try to fit in one specific category. I just do what feels right. I love DIY's because not only do I get my creative fix, but also because it feels good to look at a piece in my home and know that it was something I spent time making. It has much more meaning than something bought from a store. I think the biggest thing is just making time. It might mean sacrificing a girls' night out or a date night, but if you're truly passionate about creating, it won't feel like a sacrifice.

Lately, I've been trying to avoid mindless shopping. There was so much clutter in my house and most of it was decor/items I bought impulsively and never used. When it comes to decorating and buying items for my home, I've made a special effort to be very intentional. Instead of opting for cheaper or low quality items, I'll save my money and buy things that I love, even if it means I have to wait longer to make a purchase.

What fills your soul?

A freshly cleaned house and a lit candle on a rainy day.

Who is your mentor?

My grandmother is my biggest mentor. She taught me to read as a child and took me to and from my weekly art classes. She always encouraged me to do well in school. She always pushed me to be the best person I could be.

Share a life hack

While working as a server in college I learned that Orange Glo wood polish is great for stainless steel appliances! No fingerprints or smudges, and it looks great!

creative

CLIPBOARD

HACKS

"I had some old and well-loved clipboards, so I spruced them up with some scrapbook paper and now they look great! I used a clear coat of Mod Podge over the top to protect the paper."

@Alternativeseating

CLEVER CLIPBOARD TIPS

A class set of clipboards is one of the most underrated teaching tools out there. And they are especially handy if you want to make an effort to get outside more often. Use these tips to make traveling as a class smooth enough that it's a no-brainer when they ask to get outside for today's class.

COLOR-CODE
for grouping

Use numbered stencils to identify each clipboard in your class set. But when you paint the numbers onto the clipboards, plan ahead and choose enough colors to organize them into groups as well. Then, anytime you distribute the boards, students can gather into groups of four by color to work or complete stations.

This set had 28 clipboards, so 7 different paint colors were used. Use painter's tape and number stencils. Foam dabbers work much better than a brush for stenciling. If you use small jars of craft paint, you can dip straight into the containers to keep it easy.

Pro Tip: To get crisp edges, keep your foam dabber super dry when painting with stencils. Just dab over it lots of times with less paint, rather than soak it, or it will ooze through and make the stencil print messy.

HEADBANDS
for carrying

Purchase a few packs of elastic sport headbands. These fit nicely across the length of a clipboard, and come in handy for trapping down writing utensils while traveling throughout the school with the boards. Students will no longer drop their coloring tools on the way outside. Pens can also clip right onto these instead of having to use a string that dangles from the clipboard.

Pro Tip: These headbands come with and without a strip of clear rubbery silicone on the interior. If you choose the ones that have that extra grip, they will hold everything better, but also can grip and rip the paper, so choose carefully depending on the coordination level of your students.

ANIMALS
for partnering

Each pair of matching animals on the boards means those two students will work together. These can be painted on with stencils, or you can just use stickers if that is easier for you.

If you have numbers, colors, and animals, you now have grouping options for teams, partners, or even two large groups by using evens/odds. You'll also have the option to call out numbers to identify single students, or to determine an order for presentations. There are a lot of possibilities.

Pro Tip: Try to make each pair of matching animals come from two different color groups. This way, if you want to use both different grouping options in the same day, everyone can keep their clipboard and still work with a completely different classmate who was not in their group of four.

@how_i_teach_high_school

My classroom has no bulletin boards, so I secured clipboards to the wall with hot glue and use them to show off student work or to display pictures related to what we are learning in class. I love how they naturally frame everything that is clipped to them.

@teachtolovelearning

I wanted to be able to give my students a gift that would be helpful to them and was also affordable as I was finishing up my student teaching. I decided to order a bulk pack of clipboards from Amazon and use my Cricut to personalize them. The kids loved them!

@ReptarEm

I used Mod Podge and scrapbooking paper to create decorative clipboards.

@helping_inspire_teachers

Using folder organizers to store clipboards came to me when I had to store 20 clipboards on a very small budget. The two organizers I used fit on top of my chrome book cart for compact and easy-access storage.

getting crafty

WITH CLIPBOARDS

@msgaitherteach

I purchased clipboards from the dollar store and used acrylic paint to design them. I wanted to distinguish which one was used for various activities.

@teacherscreatingcuriosity

I put the subjects on the back of my clipboards and then place student rosters and assignment check off sheets on the other side. I hang the clipboards on the wall and they help me stay organized!

@7mapledesign

Clipboards are an easy and cost effective way to jazz up any wall space, big or small! Use them to display photos, art work, dried flowers, you name it. . . clip it up!

@girlwitha_gluegun

I wanted practical, useful holiday gifts for my department-mates. Clipboards seemed to fit the bill. A few of us have unusual names, so using my Cricut to make the gifts personalized is more special (and prevents them from walking away!).

✗ ✗

artsy inspiration from the teachers of the 'gram

natural DEODORANT

Could you live without deodorant? Probably not! Most of us couldn't imagine a day without it. But you may be starting to hear about the potential harmful effects of many popular deodorant types, possibly including your beloved deodorant brand you've been purchasing for years. It's questionable whether deodorants can truly cause harm or not, but there are plenty of reasons to be suspicious, and lots of clean options now. So why risk it?

The good news is that you do not need to ditch deodorant altogether; just switch your favorite deodorant brand to an all-natural, non-toxic one!

Here's why: Your skin is your body's largest organ. It's porous, meaning it absorbs what you put on it. When you choose a natural beauty product, you are ensuring that your skin isn't absorbing harmful chemicals into your body.

Your armpits are home to many sweat glands, have thin skin, and are close to lymph nodes, which serve as your immune system's filter. Those who shave regularly have even thinner skin in that area. Women who are pregnant or breastfeeding should be especially aware of what substances they are rubbing onto their armpits. Not only are they absorbing the chemicals, but their babies often snuggle up right in that area.

Dangers:

>> Aluminum is the active ingredient in antiperspirants and temporarily stops sweat glands from releasing sweat. However, it may be linked to many diseases, including breast cancer and Alzheimer's. Instead of aluminum, all-natural deodorants rely on plant-based powders and baking soda to help absorb wetness without any questionable chemicals entering your body.

>> Aluminum also clogs the pores so sweat builds up in your body. It also can cause a buildup of the good bacteria that actually digests sweat. This limits the ability your body has to digest any bad bacteria, making your sweat smell even worse.

>> Scented deodorants often include synthetic fragrances that could contain combinations of thousands of different chemicals, many of which are linked to serious health effects.

>> Some experts question ingredients like parabens, propylene glycol, phthalates, and triclosan.

>> Sweating is actually good for you! According to the National Institute of Health, it's a vehicle for some toxins to leave your body. Natural deodorants allow those toxins to be released, while mainstream brands do not.

How to get it right:

Read Labels
Aluminum isn't the only ingredient to look out for. There are many other synthetic materials you may want to avoid, including fragrance or "parfum" and parabens, propylene glycol, phthalates, or triclosan.

Don't give up
Some may notice an odor when first switching to a natural deodorant. It's probably just your body adjusting.

When in doubt, go with trusted brands
Research your retailer or brand to help you feel confident before you choose. For example, Earth Mama Organics creates quality, non-toxic skin and body care products for babies and for the entire journey of motherhood, and Whole Foods also publicly shares their commitment to providing quality, natural beauty products. On their website they explain, "Currently, there are 100+ ingredients common in conventional body care products that are not allowed in any body care products we sell. That includes phthalates, microbeads, triclosan, BHT, BHA, aluminum chlorohydrate and many more. However, creating a product with no unacceptable ingredients does not guarantee that Whole Foods Market will sell it. Our buyers are passionate about seeking out the finest personal care products available." Some brands make this information less accessible, which can be a red flag. Many companies are starting to help you navigate this, and we have collected a few that prioritize transparency and eliminating toxins.

Pre-Wash
Remember to wash your skin before you apply deodorant. If you don't you're essentially just covering up bacteria.

Our Top Picks:

You'll probably need to try more than one brand before you find something that can replace your old deodorant. Some natural blends are best for those who need a stronger recipe, while some cause irritation for some people, and not for others. Always stop using a deodorant right away if it causes any irritation. Try a few of these natural options to find the right fit for you, and be patient. It can take a while to adjust and detox your armpits.

Schmidt's vegan blend uses plants and minerals and comes in scents like bergamot + lime or rose + vanilla. The strength is good, but if it gives you a rash or skin irritation, quit right away and move on to one of the other options.

Native brand offers a softer solid deodorant that feels gentler on skin. It's aluminum-free and paraben-free, and can be effective for those who do not need high strength deodorant. They also have a sensitive collection for those who need a gentler formula.

Scully's "spritz" deodorant is natural and chemical-free. You'll spray each underarm a few times and rub it in. They explain that the tingle feeling signifies it's working to keep you smelling fresh for 12+ hours. It contains just three ingredients: mint oils, citric acid from grapefruit, and corn-based alcohol.

Other brands to try include *Vermont Soap Company's* organic deodorant, *Each & Every* deodorant, or *Bend Soap Company's* 100% natural aluminum-free deodorant.

Source of Study: www.ncbi.nlm.

Note: There have been inconsistent research findings. The National Cancer Institute states that regular deodorants are safe and are not linked to cancer. "Because underarm antiperspirants or deodorants are applied near the breast and contain potentially harmful ingredients, several scientists and others have suggested a possible connection between their use and breast cancer...However, no scientific evidence links the use of these products to the development of breast cancer."

by Kelly Barendt

BUILDING HABITS

BE FEARLESS IN THE PURSUIT OF WHAT SETS YOUR SOUL ON FIRE. >> JENNIFER LEE

When someone mentions a "habit," the first things that pop into most of our minds are those routines that get lots of attention and portray an extreme. When we visualize good habits, we think of the perfect model human, who exercises 5 days a week consistently, blends up a kale smoothie with flaxseed immediately afterward, and has an alarm go off to end screen time at 8 pm promptly and ensure an early bedtime. When imagining bad habits, we picture someone who bites their fingernails, drinks too much, and finds themselves out gambling week after week.

But the reality is, habits include a lot more of our daily actions than we realize. How many times a day do you hug your child? What causes you to decide that it's laundry day? How do you make the call whether to order dinner or cook healthy food from scratch? All these small in-the-moment choices are rooted in habits, because they depend on the accumulated results of the systems and connections you have set up in your life.

Small, Repeated Daily Actions Form an Entire Life

It turns out that our habits reach into our daily stresses even when we don't realize it. When you put off paying a bill, there is something behind that action. There is always a deeper reason, and it can be accounted for by the habits that led up to that moment. If you don't have the money, your spending and budgeting habits have led you to that moment. Or if you just are not sure whether the funds are in your account or not, your checkbook (or online banking) habits have gotten to where you don't have a finger on the pulse of your account. Or maybe you need to check whether your spouse paid it, or you meant to set up online billing and have put it off. Or perhaps, it's a case of intentional planning, and your habit is to deal with bills in batches on a certain schedule to avoid stress. Any reason you can offer to justify the tiny decision to set that envelope aside instead of handling it at that moment can be traced back to a set of habits that you may or may not be aware of. Some may be by design, and some you have yet to identify.

The tiny stresses of poor habits lead to repeated situations where you begin to feel just slightly overwhelmed or out of control. These moments, even when they do not consciously impact you, add up over time. The same is true for healthy habits. Their impact expands. Microscopic daily decisions come together to form an entire life.

To improve your habits, and therefore improve the entire essence of your life, you need to begin with systems. The systems you have in place will automatically determine what happens in each small moment.

As James Clear, author of *Atomic Habits*, explains, "Every action you take is a vote for the type of person you want to become." Almost everything that you do is part of a habit. If you reflect on the daily actions you take, you'll realize that each involuntary decision, including the time you leave the house, whether or not you kiss someone on the way out, and who or what you look at while you drink your coffee is a habit you have already established.

The exciting (or scary, depending on how you look at it) truth is that you change your entire life and identity by changing your habits and systems.

Identity-Based Habits

When you wish you change a habit or reach a new goal, you really need to ask yourself: "Who do I want to become?"

Clear explains that the central key is the individual's identity. One type of change is at the level of self. When working toward a new habit, try framing your goals in terms of identity over action. This means your commitment sounds like "I am a runner" instead of "I need to run for exercise." Instead of "I'm trying to start journaling online," shift your words and mindset to "I am a blogger." By saying " I am," you can increase your success with working towards the outome you want, because you are addressing the deeper level of identity behind it. Identity has power over action.

We hold tight to characteristics that we consider part of our identity. Take advantage of this depth of pride. In both desired and undesired habits, we tend to stick with whatever identity we have determined for ourselves. We self-identify based on our actions and habits. "I am a painter" holds a lot more weight than "I like to paint when I have the time." The person who takes ownership of the title is much more likely to prioritize daily routines that will include painting. But there is no line that you have to step over to officially call yourself a painter. Go ahead and say it. Own it, and now you suddenly will begin forming habits that help you live up to your identity. Tell yourself and the world, "I am a gardener. I am a Sunday churchgoer. I am a biker. I am not a smoker. I am a saxophone player. I am an early riser." Say it even if you are still on a journey to adopt all the habits that are required for the title you claim. Whatever you profess and feel internally as part of your identity, you will more successfully incorporate into your daily routines. Connect your habit goals with your sense of self.

Another benefit of approaching your habit building with a lens of identity is that you no longer have to put off the happiness that you imagine yourself working towards. Often, an outcome-based goal, no matter how acheivable, has a way of postponing the feeling of success, and the joy of the result. Most of the time, when working on building a new habit, the result cannot be seen until you've passed the key point where you either give up or persevere. In order to continue on when you cannot yet see the success of the final outcome, you need to feel the happiness of acheiving it anyway. Clear recommends falling "in love with the process rather than the product" to enjoy the journey and live a full, happy life while working toward your desired results.

The Challenge of a Postponed Reward

New habits require an understanding of delayed gratification. When you envy your neighbor's perfect garden, you are seeing the impact of years of daily habits. When it appears that your sister-in-law has lost weight overnight, she has in fact been working hard behind the scenes for six months, and the result is finally visible. The influence of a new habit coming into your life is always delayed. You'll see the fruit down the road, so relax and enjoy.

You've seen this effect before. You already know that when you neglect to address the small sneaking hints of disrespect from that one student, you may not pay for it immediately. But as the behavior grows slowly over time, you'll suddenly have a mess on your hands because you let him or her get away with it. With both positive and negative situations, the impact of small momentary decisions will end up showing up in the long run.

One Percent is Enough

This is called the compound effect. The theory is that very small choices cause a ripple effect over time that continues accumulating until those little decisions result in a very large reward. It's just like compound interest in the financial world. If you start consistently improving by just 1%, time after time, over a long period, at the end, you will be vastly ahead. The impact is much more than people realize.

For example, if you improve by just 1% each day for a year, at the end of 365 days, you would be about 37% better than when you began the year! The single percent compounds over time, and is one percent of a slightly higher number each day. This causes the slow, but powerful accumulation that allows you to improve in a growth curve, instead of just the linear progress that many people imagine when they consider beginning an improvement process.

So, if you can improve in your chosen area of daily habit by that much in just one year, the question becomes, how do you make that 1% happen?

Connect with Joy or Passion

It's very possible that the habits you wish to build

> HOW WE SPEND OUR DAYS IS, OF COURSE, HOW WE SPEND OUR LIVES.
>
> WHAT WE DO WITH THIS HOUR, AND THAT ONE, IS WHAT WE ARE DOING. A SCHEDULE DEFENDS FROM CHAOS AND WHIM. IT IS A NET FOR CATCHING DAYS.
> >> ANNIE DILLARD

into your life are ones that are activities you dread. Otherwise, you'd already have the habits and they would come naturally to you. If the action itself is something you enjoy, you may connect it with negativity because of guilt, or lack of time for it instead. For some reason, it is not already happening in your life. Perhaps you procrastinate on grading papers or folding laundry because you just dread beginning the task. Your goal may be to build habits that make these mountains stop piling up. Or perhaps you need to make a habit of daily prayer or journaling, which you do in fact enjoy. Sometimes guilt prevents you from fitting things into your daily routine because the time would have to be taken from your family or your work hours, and it just won't fit into your schedule.

Either way, in order to start making the habit happen consistently, you need to connect it with positive emotion that replaces the negativity. How can you make your grading or laundry begin to feel like a joy you look forward to? Maybe you put on your favorite guilty pleasure true crime podcast to enjoy while you fold. If it works for you, make your grading time happen in the waiting room at the salon each Friday where you show up early just for this reason, to grade with a latte in your hand, and relax while you wait for your manicure appointment.

Find a way to connect a joyful experience with your task, so it feels like a routine that you look forward to. And if you are working toward a habit that you do enjoy, but it pulls your time away from others, frame it the same positive way for their sake. Try telling your kids "Ok, it's time for my 15 minutes away in the other room. You may go ahead and begin your 15 minutes to do ..." and allow them a special time that they savor as well, doing an activity that is reserved only for that time.

If the new habit is a priority for you, set yourself up for success. Develop a system and think through these challenges before you begin. Planning will help your future follow-through.

Rewards

Since delayed gratification is difficult for humans, it helps to have some type of immediate reward. Many people give up on a habit because they cannot see the results until they work past the point of consistent success with it. Immediate rewards can be artificially added, for example by enjoying a piece of chocolate after each page you get through. But a healthier way to reward yourself is by finding ways to feel the positive impact along the way, even if it is less incredible than the

APPS

FOR WORKING TOWARD CONSISTENCY WITH HABITS

Done allows you to track multiple goals at once. This app motivates with streaks, and shows your trends over time to give a big-picture view.

Productive sets up a customized scheduled plan based on your own daily life and timing. It sends alerts to remind you and helps you track success.

Forest helps you focus on your goals to be present, stop phone distractions, and zone in on the work. You'll love seeing your digital plant grow when you're productive!

Habitbull supports self-improvement with both bad and good habits. The graphs help you visualize long-term progress while the reminders bring daily wins.

---

final reward you are seeking. To build this positivity, try recording the daily positive results when you do perform the action.

For example, if your goal is to walk up and down the staircases at school for 20 minutes during your lunch or prep period each day, you may have a chart to record the days that you do it. Instead of simply marking yes or no each day, record the positive impact that you received. Some days it may be "so proud! It felt great," while another day you might write "The exercise prevented the afternoon energy slump - yay!" Over time, you'll start to notice that you have an uplifted mood after doing the task, and that you do not receive that reward on days you neglect to do it, or can't fit it in.

The positive effects of a good habit can fade from memory when you are in the moment of putting it off or dreading getting started, so looking back at the feelings of reward may help you get moving.

If your goal is to begin a habit of calling one parent each day, the built-in reward will likely be the positive relationship with both the child and the parent. For this example, your notes may look like "She was so glad I called. We made a lot of progress in just this 3-minute conversation." Or, the reward may not come until the next day, when you see that the student has drastically improved and wants you to take notice so you can report back to the parent later.

Whatever natural result comes from the action, be sure to write it down. These will be helpful to flip back through when you decide whether to continue the habit, or whether to start dropping the ball when the motivation begins to run dry.

Routines vs. Habits

People tend to confuse a routine with a habit. Some routines do become habits, but some don't. When an action becomes a habit, you don't even think about it anymore. It is built into your subconscious and happens without having to focus. You have a routine for getting into the car, setting down your bag, turning the key, switching into gear, and backing out of the driveway. This routine has become habit. You don't have to remind your brain that it's time to turn the car on, or take the vehicle out of "park." A routine is a wonderful starting point for building a habit.

To develop a routine, choose a sequence of steps strategically, incorporating the seven motivators from Aristotle listed here. Use our "building a morning routine" reference guide at the end of this magazine to help you develop a routine. Hopefully, if you prioritize the strategies here, over time it will become a true habit and a part of your identity.

If you are the type who is motivated to "not break the chain," or if the habit you're focusing on is one you can definitely achieve every day, you may be motivated by tracking chains of success. Never miss a day! For example, if you want to begin taking a vitamin or supplement each day, set up your system to remember, and mark off every day on your calendar. You'll have nice, long, perfect chains of success. And if you ever do miss a day for any reason, the one gap is not likely to throw you off or cause you to give up completely. You'll be back into your routine for the next day.

However, if your habit is something that may not be practical to attempt to do every single day, try being more realistic by tracking streaks instead. If your goal is to do a dance workout with your daughter every night, you are likely to miss a day here and there when you are not feeling well or you have an evening committment scheduled. In cases like this, if you aim for complete consistency, the discouraged feeling when you break the chain can lead you to give up. Seeing nice long streaks of 5 days in a row, then one day off, then 6 days in a row, etc. can be a healthier approach for visualizing the progress.

For optimal success, try blending the motivation of chains and streaks together. You can track your long chains on paper, or with an app, and then when a gap happens, as it eventually will, just pick right up again the next day to begin the next chain. As long as you are also celebrating nice long streaks that do have breaks in between, you will feel the accomplishment enough to continue even after a break. Some apps will motivate you to avoid breaking the chain, while still awarding badges for nice long streaks.

CHAINS VS. STREAKS

CHAINS OF HABIT ARE TOO LIGHT TO BE FELT UNTIL THEY ARE TOO HEAVY TO BE BROKEN.
>> WARREN BUFFETT

According to Aristotle, these seven factors determine whether you will perform an action or not. Blend two or more of these to improve your likelihood of building a habit.

For example, if the habit you are focusing on building right now is writing in your gratitude journal every single day, begin with your reason, by verbalizing it to yourself and others. Then add chance by putting the journal inside your cabinet right on top of your coffee cups. You'll increase your chance of journaling because you have to remove the book before you can access your coffee in the morning. Now, you won't forget. You'll only neglect to journal because you intentionally chose not to. Now you have reason and chance both working for you in your system.

To improve your odds of success even more, find a way to incorporate one more of these seven motivators. If you can make three work together, you are very likely to perform the action. If you have a natural compulsion to log into a certain social media app each morning while you drink your daily brew, try moving that app to a further screen, and replace it on your home screen with an icon that reminds you to journal instead. Now, your compulsion will work for you. If you are on autopilot with your morning habit, you'll go to tap the app, and see the new one in the exact same place instead. Now your system is in place. You will build your habit if it really matters to you, because you have put roadblocks and prompts in your way to manage your chance, compulsion, and reason together, motivating you to perform the action you know you want to do.

SEVEN MOTIVATORS

CHANCE     NATURE

DESIRE

ALL HUMAN ACTIONS HAVE ONE OR MORE OF THESE 7 CAUSES: CHANCE, NATURE, COMPULSIONS, HABIT, REASON, PASSION, DESIRE

>>

ARISTOTLE

COMPULSIONS

PASSION

HABIT

REASON

Build a system that combines as many of these as possible, and embed your habit in that system to set yourself up for success!

Customize your own routine with our template on p.115

PAMELA HERNANDEZ

A PASSION FOR SOCIAL JUSTICE PEDAGOGY

@PHCRUZ_CRAFTING_AND_TEACHING

>> LANGUAGE ARTS TEACHER
>> DIVERSITY ADVOCATE
>> NATURAL CURL-WEARING DOMINICAN
>> HARRY POTTER CLASSROOM DESIGNER
>> CRAFTY PARTY ARTIST
>> PLANT AND NATURE LOVER

I am a proud Latina woman. I love everything about being Dominican. I love Dominican food, music, authors, and the culture in general. It's important for me to help other Latinx students embrace their Latin heritage and show that we are an integral part of this country. I am a feminist and social justice advocate. I am very passionate about social justice pedagogy in the classroom. I try to make it a point to include this in my teaching as much as I can. For example, since I teach language arts, I always pick multicultural books for my students and me to read, analyze, and discuss. This year we are reading "I Am Not Your Perfect Mexican Daughter," "Darius The Great is Not Okay," "When I Was Puerto Rican," and "Refugee." I got my masters degree in Urban Education from Florida International University. I love plants and gardening. And finally, I am a natural hair enthusiast.

text and photos by
Pamela Hernandez

I work in a suburban area. The majority of the population is Latino and Black. The demographics in my school are majority Hispanic / Latino students and African American students. Most of my students are first generation students. Most of the parents only speak Spanish and have entry level jobs. I feel that as a teacher, one of the issues is getting students to see themselves in a four year college or university. Having students be socially and financially prepared for college is another struggle that teachers are facing. Furthermore, I think teachers are struggling with how to help our students be more independent, and teach them 21st century life skills that they will need for their future.

MY PASSION

Normalizing menstrual cycles in school!

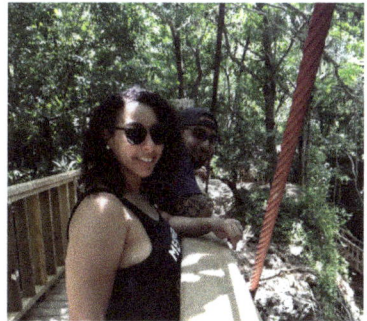

ONE THING YOU HAVE THAT NO ONE CAN TAKE AWAY FROM YOU IS YOUR VOICE

Top Tips:

> Make it a point to read more multicultural books with your kids.

> Kids won't learn from you if they don't like you.

> It's okay to apologize to your students. That lets them know you are human and you also make mistakes.

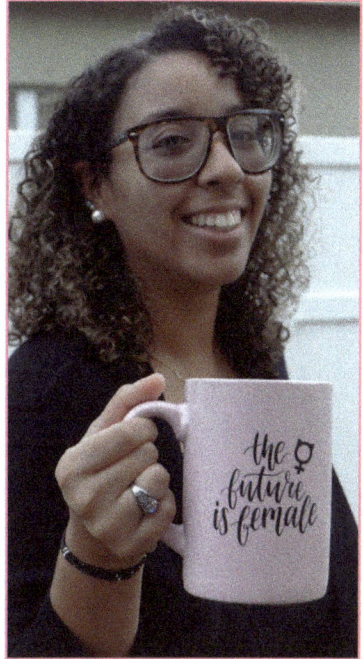

Self Care Strategy:

Spending time outside enjoying the sun and the beauty in my monstera adansonii plant, pothos, and rubber tree helps me relax and ground myself during a busy school year. I also try to meditate as much as I can. I drink herbal and green tea at night, or when I sit outside.

My favorite spot is Barnes & Noble. I could go there every weekend. I love being surrounded by books. I love picking up a random book from the shelf and sitting at the Starbucks cafe and just reading. I also like to go there and write, or grade. I love to go there for inspiration.

MY STYLE:

radical, blunt, semi casual, hood smart.

Natural Hair Masks & Homemade Facial Scrub

During the school year, I like to have my own spa days. I'll make my own facial scrub from things I already have in my kitchen, like honey and sugar. Also, I like to make natural hair masks using eggs, mayonnaise, and avocado.

Favorite Corner of the Classroom:

My favorite area in my room is my nook. I use milk crates as seating for my students. I purchased seat cushions from Ikea for $2.99 and placed them over the milk crates for a fluffy finish. I added a really nice wallpaper in that area and it gives the corner a more "homeish" vibe. That area also has different frames featuring some of my favorite plants. I also have real succulents in that area as well. The purpose of this space is to provide students with flexible seating options, and to make my classroom a space that is inviting and not an intimidating space. Students like to use the nook the most when they are collaborating with peers, doing group projects, or working in writing centers. I love plants in the classroom and in my own home. This creates a more nurturing environment. I also have moon chairs instead of traditional seating (desks).

Teacher Clothes:

My favorite teacher clothes are simply something that I am comfortable in, and a graphic T-shirt with a blazer. I love graphic T-shirts because they allow me to show off my personality. For example, I have a T-shirt that says "plant mom" and another one that says "phenomenally Latina."

Favorite Tunes

I like some of everything. My favorite band is Coheed and Cambria. However, I also really like Drake. But in the mornings I love Elevation worship.

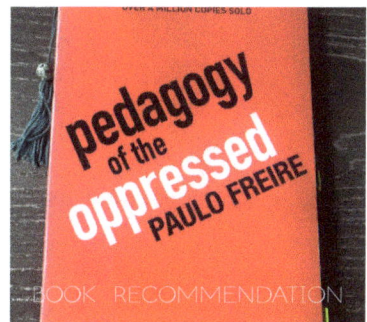

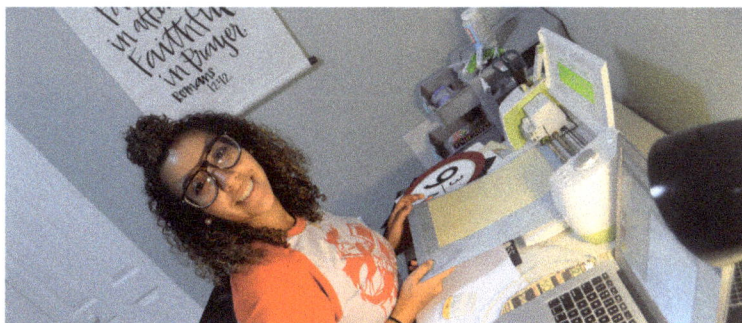

pedagogy of the oppressed PAULO FREIRE

BOOK RECOMMENDATION

TEACHER TIP:

Add some plants!

Creative passions and hobbies?

I enjoy sitting outside to work on my young adult dystopian novel, or write poetry. I also enjoy crafting and making custom products for family and friends. I'm currently working on organizing baby showers and first birthdays as a side hustle.

Favorite Teacher Lunch to Pack:

Currently my favorite lunch is a salad with baby carrots, chick peas, and baby tomatoes. I eat this literally every day at work Monday - Friday. I also add some ranch - Yum!

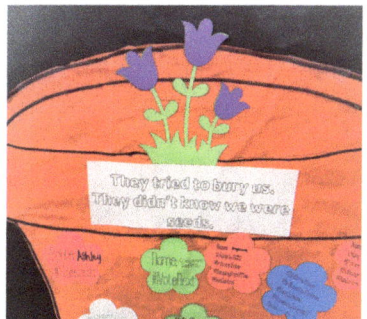

when LICE strike

by Kelly Barendt

Lice. Even the mention of these parasites makes teachers' skin crawl. Just thinking about it right now is probably already making your scalp feel itchy! Unfortunately, outbreaks of lice are common in some schools. We're here to lay out the facts, give tips for natural prevention, and give you a step-by-step for if the worst happens and you find yourself facing an outbreak. Don't panic - we've got you covered!

What are Lice? - The Real Facts

The head louse, or Pediculus humanus capitis, is a parasitic insect that can be found on the head, eyebrows, and eyelashes of people.

>> Head lice feed on human blood several times a day and live close to the human scalp.
>> Head lice are not known to spread disease.
>> Head lice are most common in preschool and elementary school children.
>> Each year millions of school-aged children in the United States get head lice.
>> Anyone in the world can get head lice.
>> Lice cannot jump, so they are only spread from head-to-head contact, (or through items that touch the head, like hats or combs, although this is more rare.)
>> The most common symptom is itching around the head. (It could take up to 4-6 weeks for the symptoms to present.)
>> Personal hygiene or cleanliness in the home or school has nothing to do with the likelihood of getting head lice.
>> The National Association of School Nurses state they believe the educational process should not be disrupted by head lice. (Children should not be sent home or restricted from participating in school activities.)

Here's what you really need

Natural Prevention

If you're in a classroom or school where head lice outbreaks are common, you're definitely going to want to be proactive and take steps to prevent them in your own hair. Here's a simple way to do this naturally:

Incorporate combing with a fine toothed comb and conditioning with a home-made spray treatment like the following into your daily routine.

DIY All-Natural Lice Repellent Spray:

Did you know that tea tree oil can help prevent lice from coming along to begin with? Mix up this blend, and be vigilant to avoid lice altogether:

Combine some coconut oil (If you're using it as a solid, make sure you melt it) with a few drops of lavender, peppermint, tea tree, and lemon essential oils in a clean spray bottle. Shake well and store in a cool, dry place. (Many different plant oils, like rosemary, citronella, and eucalyptus work well to repel lice as well if you wish to add or substitute.)

Spray and comb through wet hair in the evening. For extra prevention, spray a little onto your dry hair before you leave for school in the morning.

If All Else Fails

If the worst should happen (heaven forbid), and this dreaded situation does hit your classroom, here's what to do.

In addition to the steps above, follow these tips to stop lice in their tracks in your own classroom:

>> Remind your students to avoid head-to-head contact, or even contact such as hugging. Head-to head contact is the fastest way lice spread.
>> Encourage cool high fives or handshakes instead of hugs, and have reading time be independent instead of sharing a book.
>> Keep your hair out of reach. We know, easier said than done if you teach little ones, but it's only temporary.
>> Be on the lookout for head scratching by any students, and if necessary personally contact parents.
>> Take home any stuffed animals or soft seating, (after you check them for lice). Once the outbreak is over, you can bring back all the softies!
>> Tear out the parent checklist we've provided for you in the back of this magazine (p.114). Make copies and send them home with your kiddos.
>> Share the recipe above with families to prevent spreading. And don't worry; you'll get through this and not think of it again for a nice, long time.

natural WINES

Whether to celebrate the completion of report card comments or a successful walk-through observation, or even to recover from the stress of thinking about lice in the previous article (yep, we strategize our sequence of articles here at SnowDay mag!), teachers often enjoy savoring a glass of wine.

When you indulge at the end of a school day, you probably assume that your wine is made of natural, simple ingredients. After all, it's directly from grapes! But there's often a lot more hiding in your glass than you might think.

Wine labels are generally pretty minimalist with what they list. Here's what may be in your wine, but not displayed on the label:

>> added flavorings
>> added coloring
>> Potassium Ferrocyanide
>> Glyphosate (the active ingredient in Roundup!)

by Kate Wright
fineprintmom.com
captivatescience.com

GO NATURAL

Take time to read labels. Here are three things to look for when purchasing wine. Know the difference between these terms, and understand what each one really means.

ORGANIC: no pesticides, herbicides, fungicides, or insecticides

DRY FARM: natural rain, deep roots, rich taste

NO ADDITIVES: avoid artificial flavors, colorings, defoaming agents, and soy flower

BIODYNAMIC: grown without synthetic chemicals and with regard to the vineyard ecosystem

CLEAN WINES

Finding a wine that meets all this criteria is nearly impossible, but meeting at least one of them means you have selected a more natural alternative to your traditional bottle. Clean wine does not have to be more expensive. The demand for natural wine options has resulted in more variety on the shelves. *Our Daily Red* and *Natura* are two reputable brands that your stores may carry. Online wine dealers like *Dry Farm Wines* and *Thrive Wine* are good options because they source biodynamic and organic wines.

A French study showed that people can actually taste pesticides in their wine! Participants preferred the clean, organic wines 77% of the time.

SAVOR SMALL

Let's face it; no teacher has ever said in the morning, "I'm so glad I drank the whole bottle last night." Try savoring smaller servings. Treat yourself to a food and wine pairing, so you'll be satisfied sooner. A few sips paired with a savory snack can be just the comfort you crave after a hard day.

You also may want to consider alternatives. We all know wine is not a health food, so it is even better if you can find other options to help you unwind on some of your school days. To de-stress without a drink, try going for a walk after school, or enjoying a bubble bath. An after school yoga class can also help you relax and get to the point where you are not wishing for wine. Aim to avoid indulging after school every single day, and/or keep servings small.

MACRAMÉ
MAKES A COMEBACK

Fiber Artists Are Giving their Craft New Life with a Fresh, Modern Twist

Krystle of *Homevibes Macrame* offers patterns and supplies for fellow knotters. She hosts the Macrame Creative Club where crafters get monthly patterns, support, and a community. If you are interested in checking out her resource library, visit her Instagram page @homevibes_macrame where you'll find a link to a free beginners' ebook. Join the movement and try your hand at making a masterpiece for your own home.

Photos from
@homevibes_macrame
(opposite and top three
images on this page)

Ibolya, a creative
macrame artist in
Ontario, creates
"decorations for your
walls and plants." Find
her gorgeous flowers
and rainbows along with
other nursery and kid
items on her Instagram
@ibchy.sabo
(bottom two photos)

THE CRAFTY ORIGIN

As early as the 13th century, Arabic weavers used the term "migramah," which means "fringe" to describe the decorative macrame fibers that they hung on horses and camels. These knotted fiber artworks were not only beautiful; they were purposeful as well. In the heat of the North African deserts, the fringes helped keep flies off of the animals.

"Macrame is such an enjoyable and rewarding craft to participate in. You can use the core few knots to create such intricate patterns and pieces. It is a hobby that is becoming increasingly popular of late but still has so much uniqueness to each piece that everyone creates and that is what I love about it." >> Natasha Short, images on this page @knot.tasha

A soumak weave is a technique that gives your design a braided look when done across a few rows. It can add texture and thickness to a piece.

BRINGING TEXTURE AND CREATIVITY INTO THE HOME

FIBER ART: THE CRAFTY FACTS

MIND OF A CREATOR

Artist Demi Kahn of *Demi Macrame & Designs* shares the inspiration and emotion behind her most creative pieces.

@demi.macrame.designs

Macrame creators use nylon, silk, hemp, rayon, and sometimes even leather to build their textile art. Some artists blend more than one material in the same piece.

Contrasting the softness of a macrame wall hanging with a hard material makes it come to life. Try hanging a finished wall textile on a dowel, branch, or piece of driftwood. Add a terra cotta pot to your classic plant hanger. The macrame softens the look while the hard planter does double duty, offering beauty and utility to your home.

Adding beads will give your fiber art a groovy 70s throwback vibe, while incorporating a modern ombre dye will update your piece to give it a trendy feel.

Historians believe that macrame dates back to the 13th century. After seeing a peak in Victorian England and a surge in popularity in the U.S. in the 70s, it's now beginning to trend upward again.

Knotting techniques include basics such as the Lark's Head hitching knot and the square knot as well as more complicated knots that add interest including the spiral stitch and clove hitch.

Find inspiration from a macrame piece that catches your eye, and you'll be sure to find a tutorial out there to help you get started in this fun, beginner-friendly hobby. The macrame community is incredibly welcoming and helpful. These artists are working to provide what you need to immerse yourself in this crafty hobby.

"Many of my hand-dyed pieces are inspired by colors in the world around me. This piece (opposite page) is called the "Dinner Mint" wall hanging. Its pastel color palette is inspired by the dinner mints I used to sneak at my Grandma's as a child. I would hide in her pantry and eat half of a bag. I remember it being totally worth the inevitable stomachache. In this piece, and many others, I have also explored the combination of different techniques. This one exhibits traditional macramé, but mostly involves soumak weaving techniques and wrapping using my hand-dyed macramé rope and some sentimental yarn picked up on my honeymoon."

Demi also creates custom designs and shows her work at craft markets while running an online shop as well. She shows off her "favorite display of multiple small macramé and woven pieces that play with texture and color." (this page)

She knows that detail matters in her designs, since "each piece requires some attention as the fringe and tassels are combed out and trimmed to create the final look. Here I am trimming the pieces to keep them fresh looking after a good comb. Combing is an important part as they are meant to be experienced not just visually, but by touch as well. Each combed out fringe is waiting to be brushed and felt by curious hands.

DEMI KAHN

I began dyeing rope to achieve specific color gradients that were in my mind but that I couldn't find reflected in any rope available for purchase. I've always loved to explore color gradients in art and have enjoyed transferring something more easily applied in painting to rope dyeing. It's a wonderful way to create something that is truly unique in its creation and appearance. (top)

In addition to experimenting with dyeing, I've recently been trying to use more geometric shapes to create more intriguing pieces. This is an example of the first time I attempted this by creating fringe-full arches that are basically just begging to be touched! (bottom)

My macramé journey truly began when I decided to dedicate my creations and time to my wedding decor. I wanted to celebrate my marriage and the new chapter in my, and my now husband's life, with loved ones, but also surrounded by personal touches that were important to me. The large hangings were made throughout the last year of our engagement during many evenings and weekends of hard work. We spent the evening of our reception dancing, laughing, and celebrating beneath large macramé installations that helped create a unique and intimate experience that we, and our guests, will hopefully never forget.

In addition to creating 16 full hangings for my wedding reception, I also had this big beauty ready to go for our rehearsal dinner the night before. It is truly one of my favorite designs, with its swooping strings and textural appearance. It was a great way to open up our rehearsal dinner space and start the weekend off right with a small reveal of the macramé-themed festivities ahead. (opposite)

Follow Demi's crafting journey on Instagram @demi.macrame.designs or shop her designs at
www.demi.design

Spill coffee on your shirt? Use hand sanitizer for a quick coffee stain holdover. It won't be perfect, but will at least get you through the day, until you have time to tackle the stain!

When your whiteboard isn't as clean and white as it used to be, try using Clorox Disinfecting Wipes or Wet Ones. Test a small area first.

When taking down bulletin boards or anything stapled, don't bend down to pick up every individual fallen staple by hand! Just wave a magnetic wand over the staples on the ground.

Wipe away dirt, etc. in window tracks with a magic eraser.

Use Play doh to clean up glitter. If you don't have any, try a lint roller or masking tape.

To remove excess chalk dust from old-school chalkboards, wipe the surface down with Coca-cola.

If permanent marker gets on the whiteboard, cover the marked area with dry erase marker, then spray an all purpose cleaner and wipe. The two types of ink bond together to make the permanent one removable.

Get rid of smelly trash stench by adding a few drops of lemon essential oil to a cotton ball, and placing it at the bottom of the can. Dryer sheets under the bag work well too.

mess
remedies

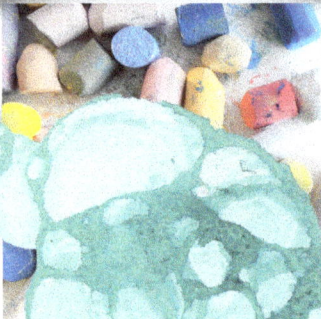

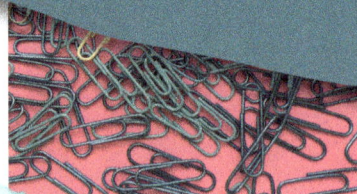

When removing labels, use Goo Gone and a scraper.

Wipe away old tape residue with degreaser.

Are you and your students frustrated by clogged glue caps? Remove the caps and soak them in vegetable oil. The oil dissolves the clogged up glue.

To get marker off of clothing, put a paper towel under the stain. Dab rubbing alcohol onto the back of the stained area, and the ink will transfer into the paper towel! You may need to repeat this process a few times.

Use felt (or microfiber cloths) to wipe fingerprints off iPads or tablets.

To clean earbuds, use a toothbrush.

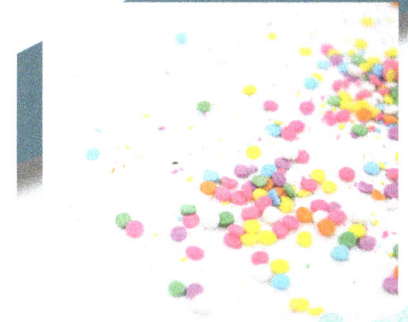

20
Clean Up Hacks for Teachers

Use sticky notes to clean in between keys in your keyboard. Then, use a magic eraser to wipe away the dirt from your laptop.

Use a hair dryer to melt gunk, like old contact paper goo off of tabletops.

For an environmentally-friendly window cleaner, try making a window-cleaning substitute combining vinegar, a bit of dish detergent and rubbing alcohol into a spray bottle.

Want to make a DIY all-purpose cleaner? In a spray bottle, mix half a cup of white vinegar, two tablespoons of baking soda and a few drops of essential oils, and use it on most hard surfaces.

Minimize germs by assigning students to wipe down certain things, like door knobs and desks, every day.

Have students wipe away desk graffiti with hand sanitizer.

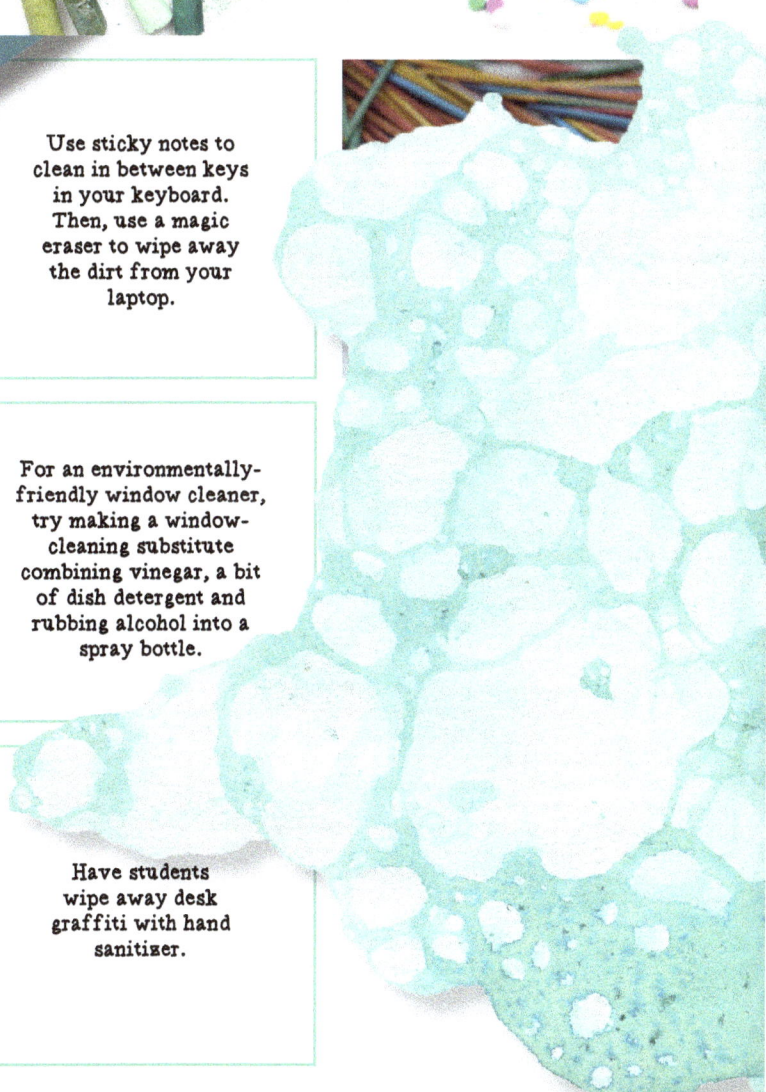

5 Ways to Style
BLACK JEANS

Black jeans are your closet's best friend. Let me explain why. If you're anything like me, you may tend to... A) feel like you "never" have anything to wear, and B) constantly be running late. Put these two things together and you will have some mornings filled with frustration! In 2019 I started buying less and using more of what I already had in my closet. I wanted to discover why I felt like I "never had anything to wear" when I had over 250 hangers with clothes on them telling me otherwise. I learned a lot of things about my style and what is necessary to purchase while going through this journey and found that having a few key pieces, plus a hint of creativity, really helped me. This allowed me to understand my style, purchase with more intention and get an idea of what I actually needed. One item I kept going back to and using as a base for most of my outfits was a favorite pair of black, high waisted denim jeans from Old Navy! I think they are different than blue or colored jeans or leggings because they give an added air of sophistication or edge to your outfit. I even started to repeat outfits and just change out the bottoms for my black jeans and I felt like it was a completely different look. Here are a few of my favorite ways to wear black jeans during the work week, on the weekends and even for a date night. Enjoy!

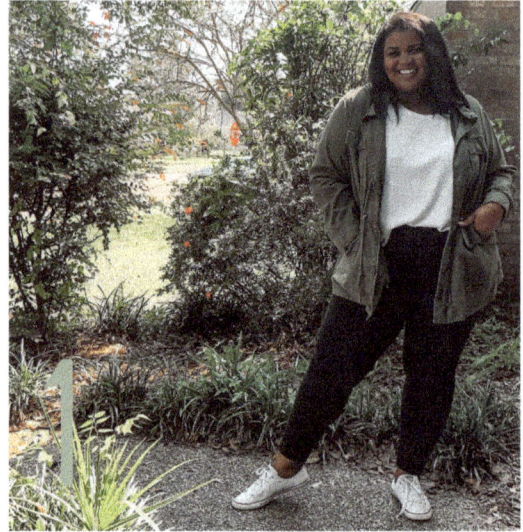

White Tee + Jacket

This is basically my weekend uniform: jeans, a white top, a neutral jacket, and Converses. It's so easy to slip on, and I feel confident and cute bopping around town while running errands, going to a student's soccer game and getting brunch with friends. If your school allows casual Fridays this could also be an option for those days.

Short Dress

As a teacher, and someone who is 5'9", I am overly conscious of the length of my dresses. I have to be aware of the wind risk with dresses and also what may happen if I bend over a little too much. Yikes! If you have a dress that you love, but you're not 100% comfortable with the length, adding some black denim will help you avoid any mishaps. It also gives you an edgier vibe than leggings. (Bonus points for denim with rips and tears!)

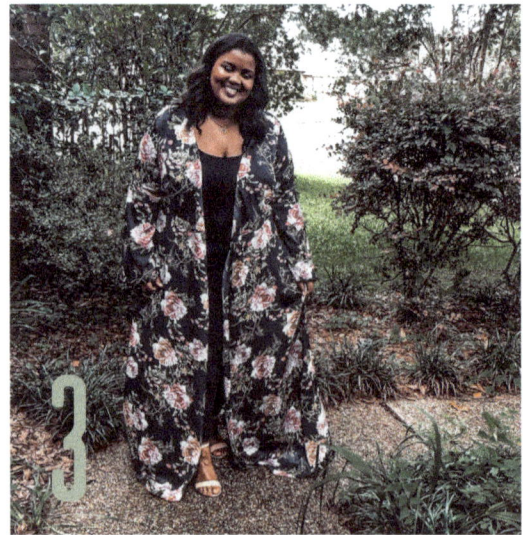

Wrap Dress

Okay- this might be my favorite, and the most unique way to take your black jeans from basic to wow! I took one of my favorite wrap dresses, untied it, and paired it with black jeans and a black tank. I tied the strings in the back instead of around my waist and got this amazing duster + kimono combination out of it. This is definitely more of a dramatic look, but I suggest you just try it out and let the rocker vibes transform you!

4

As I mentioned before, I tend to rush a bit in the mornings. I'm trying to get better at this in 2020, but until then, this is my foolproof outfit. If I'm being honest, it's quite a simple look and there is nothing extraordinary about it, but I always seem to get compliments when wearing it. A button down shirt tucks into my jeans and I add a neutral shoe. It's not revolutionary, but is just the right amount of modern and minimalistic for those days when you need to throw on something and go, without using all your brain cells trying to figure out what to wear.

Simple Button Down

This may be one of my new favorite combinations: black + camo + a touch of brown. I feel like these are basics anyone might have in their closet. You can also sub out the brown and camo for any other neutral (taupe, olive green, navy blue, cream) that you have in your closet. This outfit is basically just a combination of my most used neutrals. It's truly great for any season and a good "running around town" outfit.

"Style is the only thing you can't buy. It's not in a shopping bag, a label, or a price tag. It's something reflected from our soul to the outside world—an emotion." >> Alber Elbaz

DON'T MISS THE NEXT ISSUE

Get notifications from Snowday Magazine by registering for our emails at snowdaymagazine.com

BONUS

We will send you our free minimag too!

P. S.
Come follow us on Instagram in the meantime! >> @snowdaymagazine

candles

YOU'RE PROBABLY BURNING THEM
ALL WRONG

>>>>>>>>>>>>>>>>>>>>>>>>>>>>

How many of these common
candle mistakes are you making?

EXTINGUISHING WITH THE LID

Avoid putting your flame out by setting the lid on the candle. This will cause black smoke to accumulate inside. The smoke then is likely to ooze throughout the liquidy melted wax, changing your lovely candle scent into the smell of pure smoke for next time.

FAILING TO PLAN THE FIRST LIGHT

Wait to light your brand new candle for the first time until you have about 3 hours to enjoy it. If you do not let it burn long enough, the melted wax will not reach all the way to the edges. This will impact all future uses of the candle. Once it melts for a few hours, and the entire top layer is liquid, it will have that "memory" for future burns and melt evenly instead of "tunneling." A good rule of thumb is one hour per inch of diameter.

BURNING TOO LONG

Candles burn the carbon molecules in the air. If you let a candle burn more than 4-5 hours, it will begin to release soot into the air. This can become a hazard that builds up in a home over time. It will soak into the air, stick to the walls, and even accumulate in the nostrils.

NOT TRIMMING THE WICKS

If you do not trim your wicks, you can end up with extra smoke, burn marks on the glass container, and soot inside the wax. When the wick is too long, it contains carbon buildup from consuming more wax than it can burn off. Before lighting a candle, trim the top "mushroomed" portion of the wick off. This is best done with special wick trimmers, that catch the burned portion, but you can also tip your candle upside-down over the trash bin, and pinch it off with a tissue. Only do this when the candle is cool.

LETTING UNEVEN WAX GO

If you see a tunnel, crater, or hill in the formation of your candle wax, address it early, or you can ruin your candle and end up wasting the rest of the wax once the wick drowns or cannot reach the wax anymore. Sometimes, a nice long burn time (not more than 4 hours) can fix the situation, but if not, remove some of the extra wax. This gets more difficult the longer the problem is allowed to continue. Try scooping it out, or if you have a long enough wick, you may be able to use a hair dryer set on low to slowly melt the wax and allow it to flow across. After evening it out or removing the problematic wax, a 2-3 hour burn should do the rest.

CHOOSING POOR QUALITY

Candles range widely in quality. Sometimes there is nothing more you can do with a junky candle choice. Seek out brands that use quality soy-based wax, and choose toxin-free scents derived from essential oils. A candle with more than one wick is also generally a smart choice. This allows the entire surface to burn more evenly.

BLOWING

Blowing your candle out can spread sooty ash across your wax, leaving your candle tainted forever. Invest in a small snuffer and use it to carefully extinguish your candles.

TRASHING THE WHOLE THING

If your candle came in a nice container, save it when you're done. You can repurpose it as a paper clip cup, vase, jewelry holder, or granola jar. Place it in the freezer overnight, and then you'll be able to crack and remove the last bit of wax. Anything that is still sticking stubbornly to the bottom can be removed by leaving the jar in boiling water in the sink for a while. The last dregs of wax will melt, then eventually harden and float to the top.

YOU THOUGHT THAT THIS WAS SOMETHING YOU COULD NOT POSSIBLY MAKE MISTAKES DOING. IT'S JUST A CANDLE, RIGHT? BUT IT TURNS OUT THESE COMMON ERRORS CAN RUIN YOUR CANDLE, MAKE THE EXPERIENCE OR SCENT LESS WONDERFUL, OR EVEN CAUSE DANGERS! THESE ARE THE TOP MISTAKES WE'RE MAKING WHEN BURNING CANDLES.

In a perfect world, you wouldn't have to deal with an outbreak of lice, but alas, we all know this is not a perfect world. To make your life a little bit easier in the case that lice does strike your classroom, we've included this checklist for parents and guardians. Just tear this out, make copies, and send home with your students!

CHECKLIST FOR PARENTS

Parents and Families of Room _____,

We have found head lice in our classroom. There's no need to panic! Head lice are a common annoyance in schools. That being said, we want to stop the outbreak and return to being lice-free :) Here are some steps you should take:

- ☑ Check your child for lice or take your child to a hair salon to be checked by a professional. The same goes for you and anyone else in your household.

- ☑ Tell your child to stop head-to-head contact with other children. This is the most common way for lice to spread. If your child has long hair, make sure it is pulled back into a ponytail, bun, braids, or pigtails.

- ☑ Carefully inspect your child's clothes that he or she wore for the last two days (for lice and their eggs).

- ☑ Inspect soft household items that could be infested by lice, like towels, stuffed animals, rugs, bedding, etc.

- ☑ Make sure your child knows not to share items that touch the head with other children. (This way of spreading lice is rare, but can happen.)

- ☑ Incorporate some natural prevention, like mixing a few drops of tea tree oil and lavender essential oil into your child's shampoo. (Check for child safety and be aware of any allergies or conditions first. Consult a doctor if you have not yet used essential oils with your child.)

- ☑ You can also purchase special shampoos and rinses at the drugstore. If this doesn't help, check with your healthcare provider.

- ☑ Remember that although they are a nuisance, lice do not spread disease and are not a sign of uncleanliness. :)

BUILD A MORNING ROUTINE

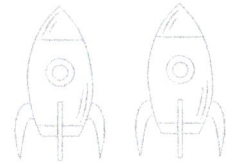

Step One:
Choose your top priorities for the focus that is needed in your life right now. Which of these habits do you want to build into your new routine? To keep your focus narrow and increase your chances of success, do not select more than three. Try one from each category below to nurture the body, mind, and soul.

Step Two:
Create your customized morning routine by choosing a sequence that will work with the reality of your morning. You may need to set your alarm a bit earlier to prioritize fitting this in. If you're unable to do that, try it in the evening. Plan the system by time blocking (use the samples as a guide). Consider which order will be most practical for your morning. Combined, the routine should take no longer than an hour, so that you can successfully implement it each morning.

Step Three:
Begin by setting up the system right away. Save your finished custom routine and place this page in the most strategic location you can think of. Set the alerts on your phone right now, and begin first thing tomorrow with your morning routine. If you realize you have missed a day, return to p. 91 right away to see which of the seven motivators is missing, and re-evaluate how you can fix the system.

1

Circle all your own priorities, then narrow it down!

Nature, Life, & Soul	Health and Body	Productivity & Work
gratitude	breakfast	grading
gardening	ab workout	cleaning
prayer	stretching	phone calls
meditation	fitness	bills & budget
walking outside	smoothies	training/education
hobby time	mental health	organizing
listening	endurance	politics
sleep	skin	screen time
self-expression	yoga	focused work
volunteering	hydration	team
conversation	strength training	journaling
back yard time	hair	mindset
plant care	mental rest	lesson planning
playing outside	cardio	side gig
family time	protein	income
craft	agility	coworker relations
self care	teeth	appointments
spouse	disease prevention	meals
art	meal planning	housework
connection	heart health	family schedule
reading	packing healthy food	laundry
(other)	(other)	(other)

2

Samples

A

priorities circled: yoga, quality time to talk with pre-teen kids, iron out family scheduling challenges

5:50 am alarm

> 6:00-6:20
> yoga

6:25 shower
6:35 wake kids

Chat with kids	Go over daily schedule. (no tech allowed)

Strategy: Let breakfast happen on the tray on my bed so they can eat and converse while I dry my hair.

B

priorities circled: cardio workout, daily prayer, self-improvement and education working toward admin. degree

6:00 alarm

6:10-6:30 treadmill	daily scripture & prayer

7:00 leave house

> professional learning to work toward degree: podcast while driving

Strategy: Do prayer and exercise at the same time. The brain only is required for one!

3

Once your plan is drafted, do not put it off. Place it strategically and begin right away.

GOD GAVE US MEMORY SO
THAT WE MIGHT HAVE
ROSES IN DECEMBER.

Inspiration from...
J. M. BARRIE

I seem too often to
be trying to catch the
wind in a net.

Would you like an
adventure now, or
would you like to
have tea first?

Never say goodbye
because goodbye
means going away and
going away means
forgetting.

The reason birds can
fly and we can't is
simply because they
have perfect faith,
for to have faith is to
have wings.

Dreams do come true, if only
we wish hard enough. You can
have anything in life if you will
sacrifice everything else for it.

The moment you doubt whether
you can fly, you cease forever to
be able to do it.

The Neverland is always more or less an island, with astonishing splashes of color here and
there, and coral reefs and rakish-looking craft in the offing, and savages and lonely lairs,
and gnomes who are mostly tailors, and caves through which a river runs...and it is all rather
confusing, especially as nothing will stand still.

Quotes from J.M. Barrie